HAUNTED
LINCOLNSHIRE

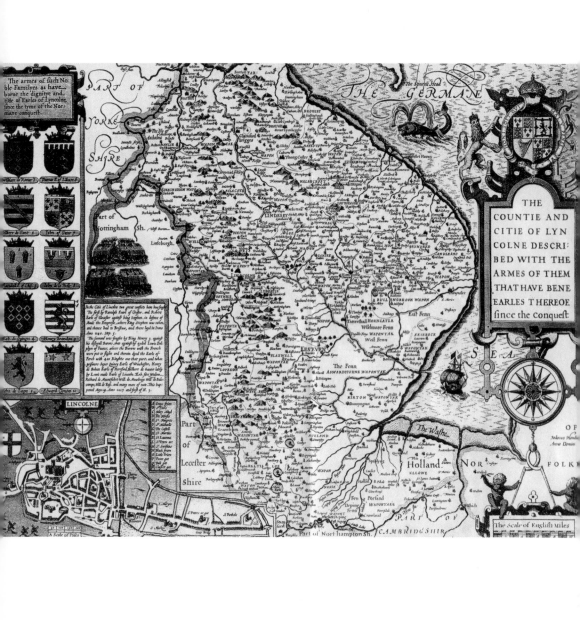

PART OF YORKE SHIRE

Part of Nottingham sh.

THE GERMANE SEA

THE COUNTIE AND CITIE OF LYN COLNE DESCRIBED WITH THE ARMES OF THEM THAT HAVE BENE EARLES THEREOF since the conquest

LINDESEY

KESTEVEN

The Fenn ASWARDHURNE WAPONTAKE

HOLLAND

The Washe

NOR FOLK

Part of Lecester Shire

Part of Northampton sh.

PART OF CAMBRIDGSHIRE

LINCOLNE

The Scale of English Miles

HAUNTED
LINCOLNSHIRE

DANIEL CODD

TEMPUS

Frontispiece: *John Speede's map of Lincolnshire, 1610.*

First published 2006

Tempus Publishing Limited
The Mill, Brimscombe Port,
Stroud, Gloucestershire, GL5 2QG
www.tempus-publishing.com

British Library Cataloguing in Publication Data.
A catalogue record for this book is available from the British Library.

ISBN 0 7524 3817 4

Typesetting and origination by Tempus Publishing Limited.
Printed in Great Britain.

CONTENTS

ACKNOWLEDGEMENTS

A great many people have helped in the production of this book, and a few grateful 'cheers' and 'ta's' need to be said.

Many thanks to the staff at the *Scunthorpe Evening Telegraph*, for their assistance with the Mac Peace story; the staff at the Lincoln Castle gift shop for their advice on Lincoln Castle's legends; the staff at Lincoln Central Library for their assistance with the archive machines; and Ros Boyce at the Lincolnshire Archives Photographic Department for her invaluable assistance in procuring several images. Mr Hallam's fascinating tour of RAF Scampton was also most useful – shame I had to miss out the McConnell tale of 1918!

Thanks also to TC, who first informed me of the one-off haunting at Ceres House, and to RS for the account of her experiences at Skellingthorpe. Also to Charlotte Wilkinson for her proofreading and information on Washdyke Lane, and Jason, Brian and Claire for their support down the pub!

Many thanks to Janet Codd for her proofreading, and Neville Codd for his assistance with illustrations and photographs.

Thanks to Bruce Barrymore Halpenny whose *Ghost Stations* contains a number of interesting stories from this area, including a version of the tale told here on page 62.

Pictures on pages 33, 41, 50, 68, 87 are from the Local Studies Collection, Lincoln Central Library, by courtesy of Lincolnshire County Council, Educational and Cultural Services Directorate.

The picture on page 52 is from the Museum of Lincolnshire Life, courtesy of Lincolnshire County Council Educational and Cultural Services Directorate.

Pictures on pages 8, 14, 17, 18, 22, 24, 29 (Gunby Hall Murder), 30, 46, 47, 55, 60, 66, 67, 70, 74, 76 (Black Dog of Hemswell) and 81 are copyright of D. Codd.

Pictures on pages 20, 26 (South Elkington), 29 Doddington Hall, 32, 36, 49, 76 (Dragonby), 79, 86, 92 (Alexandra Dock, Grimsby) and 95 are copyright of Nicola Stone. Special thanks must go to Nicola for her tireless assistance, her photographic know-how and her support, without which this project would have had about as much chance of getting off the ground as a large man running up a hill in an eagle mask flapping his arms.

INTRODUCTION

Until fairly recently, the counties of Lincolnshire, North Lincolnshire and North East Lincolnshire have been relatively ignored by investigators of the paranormal. There are, admittedly, a handful of 'classic' tales of the paranormal, including the Epworth Poltergeist, the RAF Cranwell photograph – which purports to reveal a likeness of a recently deceased mechanic amongst the line-up – and a couple of other tales, such as the Green Lady of Thorpe Hall and the Metheringham Lass, but these were all that Lincolnshire contributed to the world of the supernatural. For many, the county was a quiet, rural backwater where any stories of the supernatural leaned towards the folkloric: a land where the goblin-like Tiddy People lived just beyond sight in the Ancholme Valley, a land where a mischievous imp caused trouble in Lincoln Cathedral, and a land of ancient miracles attributed to the likes of Saint Oswald, Guthlac of Crowland and Bishop Hugh of Lincoln.

Lincolnshire had a 'dragons and fairies' feel about it; it was a county of ancient tales rather than properly presented paranormal research. However, over the last decade or so, Lincolnshire's haunted heritage has been embraced by a far wider audience and brought into the twenty-first century. This is in part due to research by a number of authors, amongst them Jenny Bright, whose investigations in *Ghosts of Lincoln* (1995) have shown that the 'ghost story' is still very much part of contemporary Lincolnshire. Such publications, for me, updated the folkloric impression Lincolnshire provided in supernatural circles, whilst at the same time illustrating that the rich vein of history which runs through the county provides the very bedrock for perhaps the most wide-ranging variety of supernatural occurrences anywhere in the UK. This is a truism to which the internet has merely added evidence, for the web has ensured that stories about the paranormal that would have once been told at the local pub are now being told to the world. In July 2005, the fifty-two-bedroom Elizabeth Hotel on Littlecoates Road, Grimsby, – whose back corridors are allegedly haunted – was visited by Living TV's *Most Haunted* star Richard Felix. Richard gave a talk to guests before taking part in a table-tipping experiment with Hull-born medium Miriam Gifford. At that event, a group of people attempted to use psychic energy to encourage the table to move by itself. This is the necessary modernising of such influential and important work of folklorists such as Ethel H. Rudkin and Miss M.G.W. Peacock.

One need only do the research to realise that Lincolnshire, a region steeped in history since the Roman era, is perhaps one of the most fascinating parts of the UK, and the modern

An engraving of Lincoln in the early nineteenth century, drawn by W.H. Bartlett.

The B1398 through Cammeringham. This scene typifies the hundreds of small communities that exist in rural Lincolnshire outside the major towns.

encounters, compared with ancient folkloric ones, raise some interesting parallels. Centuries ago they told of dragons buried at Anwick, Lissington, Castle Carlton and Dragonby; now the papers report the likes of the Wolds Panther, which became a local celebrity in 2004, and the East Coast Sea Serpent, which was spotted off Chapel-St-Leonards in 1966. Today, Satan and his cronies, who used to bedevil Lincoln Cathedral and the Boston Stump, amongst other places, have been replaced by modern-day bogeymen such as Spring-Heeled Jack, the Victorian terror who visited Lincoln in 1877, while the fairy-like Tiddy People have been replaced by a never-ending catalogue of alleged UFO encounters from the Humber to the Wash.

Volumes could be written on the mysterious history of Lincolnshire, and the study of what intrigues – and frightens – people says a lot about the evolution of society in itself: after all, as stressed earlier, most current paranormal encounters could be viewed as modern interpretations of what disturbed and fascinated people centuries ago. Is not Heather Woods' stigmata in 1992 the modern incarnation of the ancient miracles attributed to such saints as Oswald at Bardney in the late seventh century?

The werewolf of Dogdyke, the cursed 'Sack Stone' of Fonaby Top, the wild man of Stainfield woods, the list of the bizarre is endless. In 1906 the devout Ann Powell died at the hands of someone – or something – unknown in Alford. In the early nineteenth century it rained frogs in Gainsborough. Perhaps we need these tales to continually remind ourselves of our own humility and insignificance? Or perhaps we just love a good scare. Throughout the centuries there is one area of the paranormal that Lincolnshire has produced more examples of than anywhere else in the UK, and that is the ghost story. From classic poltergeist cases, to the traditional 'headless cavalier', from ghosts that interact with humans to spine-tingling tales of terror, Lincolnshire has produced some of the most intriguing and eerie ghost encounters on record.

Nor is the phenomenon of ghosts confined to draughty abbeys, castles or 500-year-old public houses. My own interest peaked when a close relative, recently widowed, told me how her mobile phone had received a call from her dead husband's phone – which was currently shut away (and naturally unused) in a kitchen drawer in her Skellingthorpe home. Mysterious shadows had been witnessed, and the couple's infant daughter had at one time pointed to a corner of a room and claimed 'Dada there', some months after he had passed on. How can such things be? This extraordinary encounter moved me deeply and left me with the impression that there were more forms of existence than merely those displayed in the mortal coil upon which we exist.

This compilation is designed to illustrate that, naturally, castles, churches and cathedrals entertain their own ghosts. But hopefully it also illustrates that this is a continuous phenomenon, with many well-documented modern day reports that our local newspapers take an investigative outlook on rather than the somewhat light-hearted approach that some newspapers might take. Lincolnshire, North East Lincolnshire and North Lincolnshire are proud of their haunted supermarkets, hospitals and shops as well as their lonely lanes and old pubs!

This book is a compilation of some of the better documented and more fascinating supernatural encounters. But there are hundreds of other stories, which space here sadly prohibits inclusion. For example, the trio of drinkers and gamblers in Holbeach, taken by the Devil, who are said to haunt the porch of All Saints Church, beckoning fools inside to join them; the Old Rectory at Fulletby, which witnessed poltergeist activity after a mysterious skull was unearthed during nineteenth-century renovations; the stone bridge over the River Slea near the ruins of Haverholme Priory, which is said to be haunted by a ghostly woman; the frightening apparition known as the 'Cammeringham Light' which was recorded as sweeping out of the morning mists on (what is now) the B1398 in the early twentieth century: and the slain Rosamund Guy who is held to drift through Irby Dale Wood, Irby-Upon-Humber. In 1912 Revd J.A. Penny received a first-hand account of another phantom woman known as the Grey Lady who drifted along Duckpool Lane in the village of Stixwould. An account appeared in his *Folklore around Horncastle*. In the 1970s came reports of a phantom train that still thundered along a disused track at Hallington. And 'Bomber County' has provided many accounts of phantom aircraft: a teenage glider was forced into a graceless landing after a near miss with a ghostly airborne Spitfire V in the 1960s above Kirton-In-Lindsey. The catalogue of ghostly yarns, old and new, is almost literally never-ending.

Read on then, and discover a Lincolnshire you never knew existed; this book will take you on a trip around the county, from the industrial north and the great ports of the north east, through the drained bog lands of the Isle of Axholme, over the vast, rolling hills of the Lincolnshire Wolds, passing by the east coast and through the ancient city of Lincoln itself, down into the remote wilds of the fens, through numerous towns, villages and hamlets on the way. And remember: unless every single witness was lying, hallucinating or mistaken, then all it takes is for just one of these tales to be true and everything we think we know would have to be rewritten.

Daniel Codd
January 2006

CHAPTER ONE

A HAUNTED CITY

What haunts the Cathedral?

Where better to start this study of Lincolnshire's ghosts than the ancient city of Lincoln itself? It is no surprise that Lincolnshire's most famous landmark, the gothic eleventh-century Lincoln Cathedral, has been the venue for some remarkable incidents in the county's turbulent past. From civil wars, earthquakes and fires, to holy men, legendary visitors and even murder, the magnificent structure has seen much activity. For example, in the late twelfth century, a sub-Dean was slain in the cathedral by a vicar whilst at prayer; the sub-Dean's servants grabbed the murderer and tied him to a horse's tail, dragging him to Canwick Hill where he was hanged.

These days, thankfully, things are a little calmer, although there were excitable scenes in 2005 when Lincoln Cathedral was chosen as the suitably atmospheric location for some of the interior shots of what in the movie, *The Da Vinci Code*, would be portrayed as Westminster Abbey. In mid-August hundreds of cast, crew members and extras took over the historic building. Hollywood A-list celebrity Tom Hanks, playing the lead of Robert Langdon, was kept well away from the public most of the time although there were sightings and quick chats with him for a number of lucky locals. On 17 August director Ron Howard took a look around Lincoln and described the city as, 'beautiful, absolutely gorgeous and friendly.' Tom Hanks himself described Lincoln as a 'lovely town, nice people.' The cathedral's famous bell, Big Tom, which struck every hour on the hour, even fell silent for the first time since the Second World War to facilitate the filming of the movie.

Such events no doubt add to the continuing mythology of Lincoln Cathedral, and although the history of this world-famous building is more suitable for other publications it does provide us with Lincolnshire's most famous tale of the paranormal. Although the story of the Lincoln Imp is not a ghost story, it serves as a reminder of the county's supernatural heritage.

In Lincoln Cathedral, high up in the Angel Choir, a mischievous little figure sits atop one of the columns. He is petrified in stone, his right leg crosses his left one, and he grins with evil intent as though he mocks all he sees. He is the Lincoln Imp, and he is probably the most famous Lincolnshire emblem in all the land.

Above: *A lithograph of the southeast view of Lincoln Cathedral, c. 1850.*

Left: *The Lincoln Imp, leering down from his pillar in the Angel Choir.*

Although he probably began life with a little help from an imaginative stonemason during the building of the cathedral, there is a history as to how the little fellow ended up in this state inside one of the greatest and most impressive cathedrals in Europe.

The best known story of how the imp came to be concerns one Remigius, a Benedictine monk appointed by William the Conqueror to oversee a diocese, which extended from the Humber southwards to the River Thames. The diocese was the largest in the kingdom, and Remigius decided that the previous capital – Dorchester in Oxfordshire – was inconvenient. Thus in 1072, the bishopric was moved to Lincoln and work began on a new cathedral. However, as the masons chipped and shifted the oolite limestone blocks and the skeleton of the great cathedral began to take shape, the activity caught the attention of the Devil.

The holy building was steadily erected on high ground, visible to all in the surrounding area, and as it grew so the Devil's fury increased. As the day of the cathedral's consecration approached, the Devil summoned up hordes of his imps to battle, and they launched an assault on the site. The workers fled in terror, but Remigius held his ground. He prayed to the Virgin Mary – to whom the cathedral was dedicated – for deliverance from the satanic onslaught, and instantly a powerful gale whipped up out of nowhere and violently threw the hordes back. In the chaos of the typhoon, one of the imps (although some claim it was Satan himself) sought refuge from the blinding wind and found himself inside the cathedral.

As the imp flew around its massive stone interior, his corruption of such a holy place caused a reaction: he petrified to stone, and came to rest where he now sits. The gusts of wind that buffet the southwest corner of the cathedral are alleged to be a reminder of this encounter, and protection against such an onslaught happening again.

Another popular variation of this legend is also oft told. In the fourteenth century, the Devil sent two imps to England to cause mischief. They started off well, sitting on the spire at St Mary's and All Saint's parish church in Chesterfield, Derbyshire – creating the famous 'crooked spire.' Then they moved on to Lincolnshire, where they darted into the cathedral and started overturning furniture. After tripping up the Bishop, they moved on to the Angel Choir but here they found themselves confronted by the sudden appearance of an angel. They were ordered to stop, but one foolish imp began to throw rocks at the angel and was instantly transformed to stone. The other imp, however, ran away during the confrontation. The imp's posture and malicious grin is often taken as an indication that he was surveying the chaos he had caused in the Angel Choir when he was turned to stone, his evil leer captured forever as if it had been caught on a photograph.

For those with an interest in Lincoln Cathedral there are other versions of this tale. Indeed, there are numerous stories of supernatural intervention and portents within the cathedral's walls, but the tale of the imp is the template for all that is supernatural in Lincolnshire. But given its history it would, therefore, be odd if the cathedral didn't entertain its own ghosts as well as the imp…

Tradition holds that the Cloisters are the haunt of a procession of spectral, praying monks. On the steps outside the cathedral the figure of a monk has been seen to turn around and wander back in through the door. And a ghostly horn sounding on the premises is supposed to be that of Bishop Robert Bloet, the second Bishop of Lincoln Cathedral.

In October 1964, scores of schoolchildren were to be found nightly staring up at the towers after a rumour spread that a small, white mass could be spotted between 7.45 p.m. and 8.15 p.m. floating quickly around the Minster. Some children attested that the phenomena took the form of white lightning that flashed from the central tower to the ground. The story was thought to have been started by senior children from a nearby school, and the sub-Dean, Peter Binnell,

Greestone Stairs, which lead one away from the East End of the cathedral.

totally dismissed the story ... but maybe some of those children who persevered after all the fuss had died down were rewarded with a sighting on one of those cold autumn nights?

More gruesome was the human head a witness reported to have seen rolling and bouncing down the hill from the cathedral. The *Lincolnshire Echo* ran the story in March 1976, but the exact location of this bizarre sighting went unrecorded.

Most of the spires and towers of the cathedral are now closed to the public because a number of people have chosen to hurl themselves to their deaths from these vantage points over the years. It is said that these tragedies have been witnessed as spectral re-enactments.

Perhaps the most famous spectre is the seventeenth-century cleric who has been spotted walking up Greestone Stairs, the exhausting climb that takes one to the East End of the cathedral. This manifestation was witnessed by three young nurses, who watched aghast as the old cleric vanished through a solid stone wall near the archway that is a feature of the stairs. The cleric may be the shade of a man who is said to have hanged himself from the archway centuries ago.

Greestone Stairs and the cathedral seem to be an area in the county where paranormal phenomena are concentrated. In the early 1990s a young woman was shocked by a ghost sighting late one summers night at Greestone Place. She reported that she was making her way home up the stairs and had reached Greestone Place; at the point where Greestone Terrace leads off to the right, the oft-reported sense of frightening unreality struck her. The atmosphere became extremely cold, and as the normal world seemed to become distorted and unreal, she suddenly noticed a woman in the garb of a nurse or nun walking nearby. Overcome with fear, the young woman stood frozen in shock when she noticed that the entity was cradling a baby, but her flowing, old-fashioned robes floated a few inches off the ground! The apparition drifted silently into Greestone Terrace and vanished. The young woman fled in fear as soon as her legs started working again.

Perhaps the phantom 'nurse' is linked to Tithe Barn – an ancient building which stands in a courtyard opposite Greestone Terrace. It is currently used by the nearby university and houses art students, but in a former incarnation Tithe Barn had been a hospital.

Tithe Barn itself is also reputed to be haunted: just one more location in a small area as rich in atmosphere and ghostly tales as it is in history.

Open the Gates!

The story goes that centuries ago a rider was sent to Lincoln Castle bearing something of vital importance – a pardon for a condemned man due to be executed. Something happened to the messenger during that desperate journey, for he never made it and the innocent man met his fate on the gallows at the castle.

Legend has it that the rider, in his haste, spurred on his mount too forcefully. Somewhere along the route the horse stumbled and the messenger was thrown to the ground where his neck was shattered. Another version of the tale tells how he stopped at a coaching inn for a fresh horse and took some time there to imbibe refreshment. One drink turned into many and he spent the night in a drunken stupor. When he awoke, day was breaking and he knew that there was now no chance of granting the urgent reprieve and saving an innocent man's life. Thus, he mounted a horse and thundered off into the early morning light, and into folklore, for he was never seen again.

It seems that the rider is destined to make the journey as a spirit, as if to make up for his failure when he was alive. Early in 1992, a young man who had just come off night shift was wheezing his way up Steep Hill at the break of dawn. Normally thronging during the day and evening, at this time of day the whole of Lincoln was abed and the young man had the silent streets to himself. At the top of Steep Hill the cobbles level out into the area of Castle Hill, with the castle itself off to the left and Lincoln Cathedral to the right. Straight ahead lay the Bailgate area of uphill, and the man pushed himself onwards, thinking in the peace and quiet only of his bed.

Out of nowhere a thundering black stallion swept past him, mounted by a rider whose cloak billowed out behind him. The pair had seemingly charged through the central arch of Exchequergate from the direction of the cathedral, and the witness had to leap out of the way to avoid being trampled down by the horse's hooves.

As he stood there in a terrified daze, the young man watched the horse and rider gallop across the cobblestones of the forecourt towards the castle gates. He heard the rider yell, 'Open the gates! Open the gates!' Then the rider and his mount simply vanished into thin air, and all was silent in the pale light of daybreak.

Lincoln Castle

When William the Conquerer reached Lincoln he found the walled remains of the upper area of the old Roman town an ideal place to build a strategic fortress. Lincoln Castle was built here in 1068, taking advantage of the River Witham, which flowed into the Wash, and the area's defensive position. Those who walk around the impressive twelfth-century ramparts these days will experience the panoramic views of the city and surrounding countryside that made the castle so vital as a stronghold of Norman rule.

On Good Friday 2004 a family on a visit to the grounds of Lincoln Castle reported a strange experience. Richard Hart (aged forty-three) and his partner Angela Allen (aged forty) had taken their two children Victoria (aged six) and James (aged four) to the Observatory Tower. It was around 10 a.m. and at that time there were no other people within the tower.

As the excited children led the way up the claustrophobic spiral staircase, a sudden cold sensation chilled Richard and Angela to the bone. The further they climbed up the staircase, the more disturbed Angela became; eventually she had to go back down after becoming extremely distressed and ill. A photograph that Richard took at this time using his digital camera reveals a strange figure. The picture appears to show a white misty shape on the stone steps – although it is somewhat indefinable and certainly bears no resemblance to the human form.

Angela herself is extremely interested in all things spiritual, and Richard feels that she may have a degree of psychic ability that allowed her to 'sense' something within the tower. 'There really is no explaining it at all,' he commented. 'It was really scary, I have to say. I won't be going there again in a hurry.'

It was not the first time that supernatural beings had spooked people in the tower: a few years previously two witnesses had reported that two figures climbing the winding staircase in front of them had mysteriously vanished when they reached the top.

On 22 March 2003 – a year or so prior to the Observatory Tower experience – members of the Bassetlaw Ghost Research Group had undertaken a 'ghost watch' at the castle. Member Paul Sims took a number of photographs that night, and when developed they appear to show semi-transparent circular white 'orbs' that seem to have been accompanying the ghost watch members as they moved about the castle grounds. Photographs of the Old Victorian Prison, Lucy Tower graveyard and the Old Victorian Chapel all show these curious little manifestations hovering in the room or scene being snapped, but some seem to show the 'orbs' hovering quite near the participants. Furthermore, film footage captured what appeared to be a sinister shadow drifting to and fro along a wall with no recognisable pattern of movement.

The main part of the team's investigation centred on the red-bricked Victorian Prison area within the castle grounds, where cameras and EVP recording devices were set up strategically. Faint but vile smells of urine and sickness were picked up by the nostrils of those present from time to time, but more unnervingly cell doors were heard to slam, keys jangled and strange muffled moaning and crying could be picked out. There is a legend that says a ghostly 'white lady' wanders around the old building: part of the complex used to contain the women's prison.

A medium brought along by the team as part of their investigation found parts of the castle extremely oppressive. During a séance in the Victorian Prison the team of eight sat round the table and were 'contacted' by the spirit of a woman named Betsy Potter who kept asking, 'What's that copper doing here?' Subsequent investigation revealed that a female inmate at the castle prison had indeed been named Betsy Potter and that she had died during her incarceration in

The imposing entrance to Lincoln Castle.

A view of the red-bricked Victorian prison building, with the battlements and the haunted Observatory Tower in the background.

The last view of Lincoln that many a convicted felon would see from the battlements of Cobb Hall prior to being hanged before the huge crowd below.

1886. A subsequent séance in the Old Victorian Chapel 'connected' with the soul of a remorseful executioner named Barclay, whom the medium linked to the mysterious 'orbs' caught on camera. Once again, investigations in the castle archives turned up an executioner from the 1890s of that name.

Cobb Hall, a thirteenth-century defensive tower within the castle grounds – and where the gallows were erected on the roof – bore witness to a terrifying ghostly encounter that is frustratingly short on detail. A lady in black appeared before a father and his son, and attempted to push the boy down the narrow, steep steps that lead to a small dungeon. The boy was saved by a grab from his father, who then watched in horror as the mysterious woman faded from view.

Legend has it that the sounds of those condemned to die on the gallows on the battlements can be heard, their footsteps sounding on the staircase as they are led to their doom, followed by the cranking sound of the lever and the slam of the trap door opening. Down the years, visitors and staff alike have claimed that yet more spectres have been witnessed: the sound of invisible horses clip-clopping across the courtyards, ghostly figures in battledress, disturbing shades of what looked like hanging people and a phantom lurcher (in life owned by an executed poacher) have all been reported through the decades.

Dining Out

The supernatural entity that is said to reside in Brown's Pie Shop has a name: he is called Humphrey.

Brown's Pie Shop and Restaurant is an old timber-framed building dating from the fifteenth century that can be found at the top of Steep Hill in Lincoln, which leads the tourist away from Castle Square and into the bustling shopping district. The name 'Humphrey' was coined by the Head Chef, who felt obliged to give a nickname to the presence in the first-floor kitchen which he often felt watching him while he worked. The chef would be so convinced that someone was in the kitchen with him that he would whirl round expecting to see them; intriguingly, although no one was ever there, his eyes were always drawn to a spot some 4ft off the floor – about the height an eight-year-old child might be if they were watching him.

There was also the suggestion that, kitchen aside, something resided in the third-floor room at the very top of the building. This room was always very cold, and on the window that overlooks the castle the name 'W. Bailey' had mysteriously been carved on the glass pane. Staff preferred not to go up to this room on their own if they could avoid it.

One day, in the kitchen on the first floor, the supernatural being threw a fire blanket at the Head Chef as he worked. The chef was furious and spun round to remonstrate with whoever was being so childish – but the emptiness of the kitchen reminded him that he was alone and that the culprit had been Humphrey. This kind of paranormal attention seeking became typical, so in order to stop it the Head Chef would take to shouting a cheery, 'Hello, Humphrey!' as he entered the building every morning. Being the first to arrive, the chef did not feel foolish, as there was no one else to hear him – only the poltergeist.

One morning the Head Chef was ill and the Manager, who was the first to arrive at the premises, set about the vegetables himself. Consequently Humphrey did not receive his customary early morning greeting, and it seemed to anger him. As he chopped the vegetables, the Manager was interrupted by the telephone ringing downstairs in the reception. So he put down the large chopping knife and went downstairs to answer the call. When he returned the knife was found several feet away from where it had been left on the chopping board; scarily, it was stuck in the floor, point-in, wobbling slightly as though just hurled there by someone.

On another occasion – again when someone else had been the first in – the Head Chef was busily working into the small hours of the night. It was the season of goodwill and the Christmas Market was due. Downstairs, on the ground floor, the front door was locked and the chef's keys hung from the keyhole on the inside of the door. Suddenly, up in the kitchen, the chef heard the front door slam violently downstairs and, fearing the premises were being burgled, he dashed downstairs wielding a meat-cleaver. But the front door remained securely locked, although the chef's keys appeared to have been hurled onto the floor by something unseen. At that point, he decided to call it a night and went home.

The Head Chef's nerve finally broke when he went looking for the Manager to ask him something. Hearing a strange clinking sound coming from an office room on the second floor, he ventured up the narrow spiral staircase expecting to find his boss there. As he ascended the steps, and his head rose above floor level, he could see straight into the office. It was clearly empty, but gradually the chef's eyes focussed on what was making the odd clinking sound – dozens of coins were floating in mid-air, and as they danced about and collided they were making the noises. As the chef looked on, in the blink of an eye all the coins collectively dropped to the floor with a great crash.

Left: *Brown's Pie Shop and Restaurant at the top of Steep Hill.*

Below: *The Jew's House Restaurant.*

This was too much for the chef, and he dashed back down the stairs and outside into the street, unwilling to return to Brown's Pie Shop for some time. The only clue to what this entity was – or is – came when a lady customer dined alone in the restaurant. The woman had a degree of psychic ability and, whilst paying her bill, she announced, unprompted, that although the meal had been first-rate, she had been a little put off by the ethereal shade of a little child who had stood by her and watched her as she ate.

Over the years Humphrey has become perhaps a little more famous than many Lincolnshire ghosts, it being not unknown to hear comments such as, 'I'm going to Brown's Pie Shop for a meal at the weekend, and to say hello to Humphrey.'

The Jew's House

At the bottom of Steep Hill, Lincoln, can be found the Jew's House. Today it houses a fine restaurant but it is one of the oldest houses in Europe, a splendid example of domestic Norman architecture which reflects the affluence of Lincoln's Jewish community of centuries ago. It was once the residence of Bellaset (or Solomon) of Wallingford, who, in 1290, was hanged for clipping the king's coin (forgery). It also neighbours the house where the little boy named Hugh was murdered in 1255, a crime blamed on Lincoln's Jews.

The Jew's House is allegedly haunted by spirits that inhabit the top floor and the attic, and mysterious footsteps have been heard thumping up the staircase. A couple of tourists once took a series of photographs of the exterior of the Jew's House; the second one of three shots appeared to show a kind of spectral knight in armour standing outside the building.

The Theatre Royal

Most theatres in Britain have their famous superstitions and almost as many claim to be haunted. Lincoln's Theatre Royal is no exception. In the mid-1970s a member of staff at the Royal was put out by the smell of cigar smoke that reached his nostrils during an afternoon matinee sitting. He spotted the culprit – a strangely out of place portly gentleman with a large moustache who sat at the back of The Circle, on his own and several rows behind all the other customers. Smoking was forbidden in the theatre, in part because of a devastating fire that had burned the old Theatre Royal down in the late 1800s. The staff member made his way to the back of The Circle to ask the man to put out his cigar; but when he got there the man had somehow vanished into thin air: there was no smell of cigar smoke when the air should have been thick with it, and the other patrons did not seem to have been disturbed by any such smell. The man could not possibly have stood up without being spotted by the staff member. However, there was a single, tantalising clue; the seat where the man had been was in the 'down' position, while the rest in the row were 'up'. Someone had been sitting there…

The vanishing man had been sitting near a blocked-up, decades old doorway, and the whole thing is reminiscent of some kind of 'time-slip' incident. Maybe he walked through the old doorway and somehow stepped back into his own dimension without ever realising anything

The Theatre Royal.

was amiss. Whatever the truth, the area is now known to staff as 'the haunted corner'. On another occasion, perhaps a whole group of phantom theatregoers 'time-slipped' – for staff in a different part of the building heard a 'bang' come from the auditorium. When they dashed there to investigate, they found *all* the seats in the auditorium down as though occupied by an invisible audience; yet the theatre wasn't even open.

The County Assembly Rooms

Sometimes it seems that every building in Lincolnshire has its own resident ghost. At the County Assembly Rooms in Bailgate, Lincoln, they take a more traditional form. The place was built in 1745 and is used for various functions – including the meetings of the local Freemason's lodge. In days gone by one of the dining rooms used to be a card room and there are held to have been several murders there linked to cheating allegations. Some of the waitresses are too frightened to go down to the basement on their own on account of the strange noises that can be heard emanating from it. The resident ghost appears to be a man dressed in the outfit of Cavalier times.

He was spotted by a waitress in the doorway to the ballroom, where he simply vanished. It has to be wondered how a building erected in the year of the Jacobite Rebellion came to have a ghost apparently from a time period 100 years earlier.

Mysterious talking has also been reported in the place when no one is around, and objects have been moved around by some invisible force. The Lincs Paranormal Research Team thought the County Assembly Rooms had a good enough pedigree to warrant an investigation, and they did indeed experience this latter phenomenon for themselves: for a crate apparently moved itself from one spot to another. Sadly the team did not manage to capture evidence of this with their equipment.

In 2005 the Lincs Paranormal Research Team carried out a second investigation there, setting up digital cameras, Dictaphones, thermometers and holding séances. During one séance in the ballroom at 2.35 a.m. the team reported hearing murmuring noises and the sound of heavy furniture being moved around upstairs. They also experienced sudden cold spots, together with a door being found unaccountably opened; a tap also mysteriously turned itself on. Two of the pieces of camera equipment also malfunctioned, leading the team to agree that there was, indeed, a presence at the County Assembly Rooms.

Just Passing Through

The strange experience of a handyman at Ceres House, on the northern outskirts of Lincoln, indicates that even the erection of a modern building cannot stop the passage of spooks. Ceres House is a relatively new building, built in 1977, and today is a busy place housing several governmental departments. These days the large, main room on the ground floor that faces out onto Nettleham Road is full of civil servants, but in the mid-1980s that large room was an all-purpose filing room stacked with documents and records.

Tony, the handyman in question, had retreated to the solitude of the room for a quiet cup of tea. It was fairly early in the morning and he sat in a chair with his feet up on a desk, pouring himself a cup of tea out of a flask.

Tony's reverie was interrupted by a curious misty shape that manifested itself over by a far wall, as though it had appeared in the room *through* the wall. It drifted across the floor, and, as Tony watched, it was briefly obscured by one of several pillars that were in the room. Then it reappeared once more, continuing its weird way across the room. Once more it was obscured by a pillar, once more it reappeared … and then Tony lost sight of it, as the angular corner of one of the walls in the L-shaped room obscured it from his vantage point.

Recovering from his amazement Tony leapt off his chair and rushed to the area of the room where he had last been able to view the shape. It was no longer visible, presumably having traversed the room and vanished through the opposite wall. The temperature at the spot were Tony now stood was extremely chilly, in contrast to the spot were moments before he had sat with his tea.

Tony was adamant that what he had seen was the shade of a human being, but so misty and ill-defined that it had been impossible to make out any details – even as to whether it had been male or female. But Tony had certainly seen something, and he immediately raced to get one of the managers to report the incident. Taking her to the room, she too felt how the air became strangely chilly at the point where the entity had made its way.

Ceres House, a modern building that a ghost apparently drifted through.

This incident, for all its vagueness, is truly strange, not in the least for taking place in daylight. It is the kind of tale that one feels is simply too *dull* to be made up. In other words, if one were going to invent a ghost story, they would certainly add details such as tricorn hats, or rustling dresses or some other such thing. But for twenty years Tony stuck to his account of what he had seen, never elaborating on any details of the thing other than reiterating that he was sure the form was that of a human.

Ceres House is too young to have a ghost linked to the building, so it is likely that this spectre falls into the category of the 'action replay' type of ghosts, maybe a spectral echo of someone who perhaps travelled over the spot when it was merely a rough track leading away from the city, possibly centuries ago. The ghost has not been seen since.

In cases such as this it can be said that the lack of detail in no way detracts from the believability of the tale; some might even argue that it adds to the credibility of the account.

CHAPTER TWO

GHOSTS ACCUSTOMED TO STYLE

The Green Lady of Thorpe Hall

The origins of the spectre that haunts Thorpe Hall at South Elkington have over the years become confused in the telling; but whoever tells the story, the basic ingredients are always there: a lost love, and a tragic death.

Thorpe Hall is an Elizabethan building that stands on the outskirts of Louth, and owes its present form to Charles Bolle who rebuilt it in 1690. But the story of the Green Lady dates back a hundred years before that, when Charles' great-grandfather, Sir John Bolle, lived in the hall towards the end of the sixteenth century. Sir John was knighted by Queen Elizabeth I for his conduct at the battle of Cadiz, Spain, in 1596, where a combined English and Dutch force sacked the wealthy port. The events that brought about the story of the Green Lady are said to have happened in this year, although other versions have it that it was during a raid in 1587 that the incident took place.

During the campaign, Sir John Bolle was captured by the Spanish and imprisoned in a dungeon in Spain. There, on a daily basis, a wealthy Spanish noblewoman called Donna Leonora Oviedo passed by his cell as she walked in the street, and eventually she stopped to talk to the English prisoner through the bars of his cell window. Thereafter she began to bring him food so that he would not starve to death, and gradually she began to fall in love with him. Eventually she gained Sir John's freedom by bribing his gaolers with jewellery, and then produced more treasure for Sir John to be able to get back to England. All she asked was that he take her with him.

Sir John, although happy to accept Donna Leonora's help, refused to compromise himself and take her back to Thorpe Hall with him. At first, he tried to dissuade her by saying that the sea journey would be too much, but finally he had to confess that he already had a wife and family back in Lincolnshire who longed for his return. The heartbroken Spanish noblewoman agreed that she could not accompany her love back home. An alternative version of this incident

Left: An *engraving of Sir John Bolle.*

Below: *The countryside of South Elkington, adjacent to Thorpe Hall, where the Green Lady is said to sadly wander.*

says that during the battle Sir John was assigned a prisoner: he was astonished when it turned out to be a member of the Spanish nobility, Donna Leonora. He treated his captive kindly, and ultimately the maiden fell in love with the English knight. She offered him jewels to take her with him back to England, and eventually Sir John was forced to admit that he had a family waiting for him.

The next piece of the story seems universally accepted. Donna Leonora insisted that her unrequited lover kept all the jewels she had given him, and that he took them back to England as presents for his wife. The Spanish noblewoman also begged him to take a portrait of her with him – so that he would never forget her. She handed him a small image of herself, on a wooden panel in a gilt frame; Donna Leonora wore her finest green dress in the image, and was playing a guitar surrounded by ladies-in-waiting.

Sir John returned to his Lincolnshire home and hung the portrait in Thorpe Hall. The Spanish lady's kindness left a lasting impression on him, for he started the bizarre custom of laying a place for Donna Leonora at mealtimes – a routine that was still being performed in the 1920s.

What became of the lovelorn Spanish maiden remains unclear. Some say that she took herself away to a nunnery; her valuable treasures no use to her any more after her heart had been broken. Others say that the poor woman killed herself after watching Sir John's ship sail away from Cadiz and back to England.

However, there is another version of the ending. Donna Leonora could not forget her Englishman, nor stop loving him, and her torment ultimately drove her to leave Spain for England to seek him out. Once she had made her way to Lincolnshire she donned her green dress and made her way up the drive to Thorpe Hall. As she neared the hall, she heard laughing and merriment from within, so she ducked into a hiding place behind some trees. There she observed Sir John and his wife and family as they enjoyed an evening meal. Realising that it would never be, Donna Leonora drew a dagger and stabbed herself to death underneath an oak tree.

Sir John Bolle died at Thorpe Hall on 3 November 1606, and with him died the only first-hand account as to most of these events.

However, the portrait of the Green Lady continued to hang at the hall and look down upon its occupants, gently smiling at them. A place continued to be set for her at the dining table, ensuring that her presence was felt for decades, long after the Bolle family had been forgotten. However, the portrait was sold in 1760, and nowadays its whereabouts are lost to the ages. The sale of the portrait may have inspired Thomas Percy to include the tale in his *Reliques* (1765), which includes a ballad called 'The Spanish Lady's Love'.

But the Green Lady allegedly still resides at Thorpe Hall, in ghostly form. The gardens and road adjacent to the hall are the haunt of the heartbroken spectre, where she allegedly glides across the Elkington to Louth road. She wears her fine green dress, and one of her favourite sites is an impressive sycamore tree with five trunks known as 'The Five Sisters' in the deer park. In the late twentieth century the owners of Thorpe Hall claimed that there was an indication of a handprint in the wall at a handgate near her favourite point for drifting on and off the property.

Why should the Green Lady haunt Thorpe Hall? It is unclear, but if she does perhaps it adds weight to the tale that she killed herself in the grounds all those centuries ago. Or perhaps it is just as likely that she periodically turns up for the meal that successive owners have symbolically prepared for her down the years. Maybe there is a connection to the portrait that no longer hangs at the hall. Or maybe, lost love can cross both dimensions and oceans.

Haunted Halls

Just west of Lincoln is Doddington, famous for the splendid Doddington Hall which was completed in 1600. The hall has been occupied since then but is open to the public; and it is supposedly haunted by a Brown Lady, who appears to new brides staying at the hall. The Brown Lady manifests herself in one of the bedrooms and will smile at the new couple as though giving them her blessing before disappearing.

Far more shocking is the spectral re-enactment of a brutal incident in the hall's history, when a girl threw herself to her death from the roof whilst being pursued by a lustful squire. The wraith screams in terror as it falls from the roof, and this ghastly scene is alleged to be replayed every autumn.

Gunby Hall, built in 1700 by Sir William Massingberd at Burgh-le-Marsh, west of Skegness, is also allegedly haunted. The ghostly outlines of two young lovers have been witnessed drifting along a path that passes a pond in the grounds of the 500-acre property. The sightings are usually accompanied by a sensation of deathly cold, but this leaves the witness after a few seconds when the apparitions fade and disappear. The sightings seem to be linked to rumours of a brutal murder that apparently occurred some time during Sir William's residency at the hall.

Sir William discovered that his daughter (some accounts have it that it was his wife) was about to elope with one of the servants, a postillion. On the night that the lovers intended to flee, Sir William hid in waiting and when he saw the postillion he shot him dead. The poor servant's body was dragged through the grounds and thrown into the pond. Some versions say that Sir William was so enraged that he then shot his daughter dead as well.

Perhaps word of the secret murder got out into the surrounding countryside somehow, for soon locals were whispering that Gunby Hall was cursed and that no male of Massingberd's descent would ever inherit the house. Worse, the ghostly form of the murdered servant was seen, haunting the path by the pond in an eternal wait for his lover who would now never arrive; however, perhaps the reports that two spectres haunt the path bear out that the two doomed lovers did indeed meet again – in the afterlife. The stories of these spirits led to the path being called 'Ghost Walk'.

The grim discovery of a child's skeleton found in a hollow tree in the grounds of Cadeby Hall, north of Louth, seemed to add a grain of truth to the old rumour that, years earlier, a seven-year-old boy had vanished while playing – and the child's vengeful mother had cursed the hall. The place is reputedly haunted by the shades of figures that look like monks – it is thought Cadeby Hall was once the site of a monastery.

Spalding is the location for the fine Welland Hall, and, like some other stately homes in this chapter, it appears to have been the scene of a murder committed behind a veil of secrecy that the wealthy often enjoyed. It is clear that few of these crimes mentioned here came before the courts, and may have leaked out from behind the exclusive walls in the form of rumour, accounting for the sometimes confusing details. At any rate, the master of Welland Hall murdered his wife in an upstairs bedroom, it is said, and then killed himself by jumping out of one of the upstairs windows. A different version claims his wife murdered him when she discovered he was having an affair with a servant girl. Either way, it is his spirit that drifts through the stately rooms and corridors.

Welland Hall later became Spalding High School, and the girls there named the resident spectre 'Boris'. It seems they were not frightened by the entity, and he became such a fixture that in the 1920s the senior girls organized 'Boris hunts' as a bit of Christmas fun for the younger

Doddington Hall.

The murder at Gunby Hall.

Nocton Hall in 2005, a year after the devastating blaze swept through it.

girls. This is at odds with the allegedly brutal life of 'Boris' – and some staff members were wary of the fun and games, especially when they reported that some rooms in the hall contained an extremely threatening presence.

A ghost known as the White Lady is said to wander the rooms of Ayscoughfee Hall, originally built in the 1420s for the local wool tycoon Richard Alwyn on the banks of the River Welland, Spalding. The hall is now a museum and tourist information centre, and over the years staff have reported a ghostly sensation in the rooms and galleries.

The Victorian Nocton Hall, near the village of Nocton, southeast of Lincoln, fell into disrepair after its usage as an RAF hospital and then a residential home, but prior to this it was once home to Frederick Robinson – Viscount Goderich of Nocton, and Prime Minister in 1827. Presumably occurring during this era, there is a story that a wayward son of the house brutally raped a serving girl and then murdered her when he found that she was pregnant.

Decades later, when Nocton Hall was transformed into an RAF hospital, it was said that a particular room in the building was haunted by this tragic girl's ghost On some three occasions, nursing officers sleeping in this room claimed that they had been woken in the night – always at 4.30 a.m. exactly – to see an apparition standing before them.

In October 2004, seventy fire fighters were called to a blaze at Nocton Hall, but could not save it from being destroyed. Arsonists were blamed; perhaps the spirit of the slain servant girl was laid to rest with the building's own death.

Glentworth is a small village that lies about twelve miles north of Lincoln, and Glentworth Hall, built in 1566, fell into disrepair after the Second World War. Through the decades, for some unknown reason, the hall gained a reputation with the locals for being haunted.

Before the war, the hall came into the possession of Elizabeth Green, who recalled years afterwards how the house seemed to have a kind of supernatural aura; there was a strange sensation among those who lived there that 'something' was watching them, and bolted doors were often found mysteriously unlocked the following morning. Outside, curious lights sometimes shone through the windows. The Green family eventually moved out when the hall was bombed by a German aircraft.

In 1946 the third storey of the hall was removed and locals say that this allowed trapped spirits to leave their earthbound prison. Glentworth Hall was saved from total abandonment and ruination in 2000, and has been superbly renovated.

Gainsborough Old Hall

In Gainsborough, near the River Trent, stands the huge manor house called Gainsborough Old Hall, the foundations of which date back to at least the thirteenth century. The building as it stands now dates from the late 1400s and over the centuries the great hall and it's sturdy castle-like tower has hosted many famous and notorious names: in 1482, minstrels played throughout a banquet attended by King Richard III; in 1541 King Henry VIII stayed, and rumours since have speculated that he met Catherine Parr (his sixth wife, who outlived him) during his visit. In the 1700s the Methodist reformer John Wesley preached there on a number of occasions.

The three-floored polygonal tower was added to Gainsborough Old Hall in 1483 and is haunted by the Grey Lady, thought to be the daughter of the Lord of the Manor who fell in love with the heir to the Talbot family of Torksey. Although the Talbot family was well-to-do, the son was a soldier and considered not good enough for the young noblewoman. However, using her maid as a go-between, the lovelorn young lady planned to elope with her soldier. One evening he sent a boat up the River Trent to take her away; but the plan was discovered and foiled by the Lord of the Manor.

The young girl apparently took to confining herself in the tower, a self-imposed exile brought on by her broken heart and her father's anger. A more sinister version claims her father had her locked away in the tower to end forever her relationship with young Talbot. The poor girl is said to have eventually died in the tower, having pined away on her own. Whatever the truth, over the years a legend grew that the unhappy child still wandered the tower, endlessly waiting for her lover to arrive. The ghost became known as the Lady in White.

Perhaps the shade of the spirit has dimmed through the centuries, for she is now known as the Grey Lady. Her otherworldly appearances are rare – but when she does put in an appearance, she does it in style. In the early 1800s a tradesman employed to paint the hall was found laid out semi-conscious in a state of abject terror, and kept repeating, 'She is there!' The young man spent the next few days half-insane, but when his brain fever cleared he claimed that the Grey Lady had appeared out of nowhere, dressed in white and smiling at him. She had beckoned him as though to follow her through the wall, but he had simply stood there with his mouth open aghast. This seemed to annoy the spirit, and the young painter gradually slipped into a frightened stupor before passing out.

Gainsborough Old Hall.

These days the Grey Lady seems to restrict her presence to ghostly footsteps, and the sound of a door closing in the hallway leading to the tower – a psychic echo, perhaps, of her shutting herself away in her lonely exile. Shaun Clark, the Heritage Assistant at the hall, has heard such sounds. But in the 1960s another tradesman briefly caught a glimpse of a shadowy figure vanishing through a wall: subsequent renovation at the spot revealed that behind the plaster panels was a filled-in doorway – which 200 years earlier had led to the tower bedroom.

Shades of the High Life

Some spooks appear to have a taste for the good life, and appear unwilling to desert the county's stately homes.

Harlaxton Manor at Harlaxton, south of Grantham, was built between 1832 and 1844, and is nothing less than exceptionally impressive. The mixture of styles – Jacobean, Elizabethan and Baroque – presents such a gothic atmosphere that the house was used as the exterior for the film *The Haunting* (1999) starring Liam Neeson and Catherine Zeta Jones. Since 1971 the manor has been Harlaxton College, owned by the University of Evansville, Indiana. But in-between terms, when the 160-odd students have returned home to their friends and families, and the palatial interior lies silent, it is said that the manor echoes with the screams of an infant who long ago died a horrific death.

Some say that the child who died all those years ago was merely 'murdered'. Another story tells a far more graphic and tragic tale.

A servant was nursing a baby to sleep in a certain room in Harlaxton Manor known as the Clock Room, in front of a roaring open fire. The servant fell drowsy in her chair, and the baby rolled from her lap and into the fire, where it burnt to death, screaming in pitiful agony.

If such an event *had* happened, even 150 years ago, there would have been some record of it occurring – but there is not. Nevertheless, visitors have reported being chilled to the bone by phantom baby cries in the room where tradition says the tragedy happened; some have even reported hearing terrifying screams.

And that is not all. The Clock Room is also haunted by a Woman in White, alleged to be the eccentric Violet Van der Elst (who owned Harlaxton between 1937 and 1948), and a mysterious dark-robed and hooded monk-like figure. A mysterious man dressed all in black – who appears to be distinct from the monk – also wanders the manor.

Three miles northeast of Grantham is Belton House, built in the shape of an 'H' in the 1680s and decorated in virtually every room with portraits of descendants of the original owner of the estate, a wealthy Elizabethan lawyer. It is one such wall decoration that is the focus for a unique haunting: although the details are frustratingly confused.

The phenomenon took the form of a mark that appeared on the framed family tree which hung on a wall in a corridor near a bedroom – on the underside of the protective glass that covered the heirloom! This fact seems to be agreed on. Tradition holds that the bedroom in question belonged to Lady Alice Sherald, who lived at Belton House in the early 1600s. In the

Harlaxton Manor: a photograph taken in the early 1900s.

1980s a nearby portrait of Lady Alice was removed from the stately home to be taken to London to be professionally cleaned. It was at this point that the marks began to appear underneath the glass on the family tree, gradually taking the distinct shape of two handprints. They remained there for weeks – until the portrait of Lady Alice returned to Belton House and was re-hung; then they faded away.

So goes the story. However, another version of the story claims that the mysterious marks formed the outline of a lady in period costume, and within a day a slender neck adorned with a fine necklace could be observed. The image further defined itself to reveal shoulders and hands, but the spontaneous manifestation remained headless.

Whatever the truth, Lady Alice is reputed to appear herself quite regularly. Her spirit is known as Belton's Bright Lady and she haunts the main staircase hall. Another spectre that is reported as often appearing at the house is that of a tall, dark man dressed in a dark cloak. He appears in the Queen's Bedroom, and one wonders if he had the good grace to stay away when King William III used the bedroom during his visits to the stately home in the late 1600s!

CHAPTER THREE

HAUNTED HOMES

Old Jeffrey

The poltergeist that plagued Epworth Old Rectory in the eighteenth century is among the best ever documented cases – for the ordeal was chronicled by one of the family's children, none other than John Wesley himself.

Long before John Wesley was to become the founder of the Methodist church, the Wesley household – consisting of the Revd Samuel Wesley, his wife Susanna, their sizable brood of children and the family servants – arrived at Epworth Rectory in 1696. John was born at Epworth in 1703 where his father held the position of rector in the small North Lincolnshire town in the Isle of Axholme, eight miles south west of Scunthorpe. In February 1709 there was almost a tragedy at the rectory when sparks from the fire started a blaze late one night; young John was the last to be plucked from the burning house, with only seconds to spare.

This dramatic event preceded further unfortunate incidents. In 1716 something wholly supernatural invaded the parsonage and the family underwent a two-month nightmare which, although chronicled almost three centuries ago, remains one of the most compelling and disturbing accounts of a poltergeist manifestation ever recorded. Although John – at that time aged thirteen-and-a-half – was away from the rectory during the terrifying outbursts, the other family members chronicled their experiences and eventually John collected all their written accounts to faithfully compile the events of the supernatural invasion at Epworth Rectory. His father's account of what took place was entitled, *An Account of noises and disturbances in my house at Epworth, Lincolnshire, in December and January 1716.*

The family had returned to a rebuilt Epworth Rectory in the wake of the blaze, and all was calm until the winter of 1716. On 2 December that year a manservant named Robert Brown was disturbed in the night by repeated, violent rapping at the front door. More than once he ventured from his bedroom to answer, but whenever he opened the front door there would be no one there. Returning to his bedroom, Brown blamed the incident on children playing tricks; but within hours it became apparent that *something* had got into the rectory. As he lay

Epworth Old Rectory, bedevilled by a poltergeist in the eighteenth century.

in bed Brown listened aghast as an unseen entity moved around the room making a noise that sounded like the gobbling of a chicken. He was also to see, it is claimed, a corn-grinding hand mill turning on its own.

The following morning Brown cautiously told one of the maids what had happened and received scorn for his trouble. But later on the same maid was disturbed by a furious knocking on the door as she was writing her diary, and the experience so frightened her that she fled in terror.

John's twenty-year-old sister, Molly, was the next to experience something weird. As she sat reading in the library the door opened on its own accord; the sound of footsteps entered and walked around Molly's chair, accompanied by what sounded like the rustling of a silk dress. One after the other, family members came forward to report their own eerie experiences. Another sister, Emily, had heard a cradle being rocked forcefully in one of the bedrooms where there was no such cradle: this wasn't hysteria taking effect either – for her mother, Susanna, had been there and had heard it too. Further stories followed of mysterious rapping sounds on a table, loud bangs in the kitchen and hall, and phantom footsteps on the staircase. The first sign that something was amiss, before the servant Brown claimed his experience, had been 'several dismal groans' followed by strange knocking, and a sinister cackling noise was also reported. At 9.45 p.m. every night the entity's footsteps were to be heard plodding down from the north-east corner of the rectory, and Emily Wesley christened the invisible force 'Old Jeffrey' after an old man who was said to have passed away in the place before the Wesley's time there.

Within a short time the poltergeist's activity became far from hidden, becoming a collective experience suffered by the household. For instance, young John recorded how a knocking would interrupt Samuel Wesley nightly after he had gathered the family for prayer. It would become thunderous and reach a crescendo as Samuel reached the 'amen'. On other occasions the family would hear bottles smashing in the pantry – but when they checked, everything in the pantry would be orderly and intact. Samuel Wesley's account also told how 'One night when the noise was great in the kitchen', a 'door in the yard' (which was often to be found unlatched) was held closed by his daughter Amelia. The door still managed to unlatch itself, and then swung violently inward against her, although on inspection there was nothing on the other side that had forced the door. The poltergeist also appeared to taunt household members personally: often, nine very loud knocks were heard very near Samuel Wesley's bedstead.

By this time strange things were also being seen within the rectory. Various members of the Wesley household, including servants, claimed that a strange, old man in a white gown had startled them. This ghostly shade was witnessed by a daughter, Hetty, who told her parents that 'something like a man' had drifted down the stairs while she sat waiting for her father. She was so frightened that she fled the room. Mrs Wesley herself saw a phantom white badger, without a head, underneath one of the girl's beds. It seemed to vanish under one of daughter Emily's petticoats. And the servant called Brown claimed a white rabbit had darted out of the kitchen fire. He had seen the mysterious creature earlier in the dining room; he had chased it with a candle but had lost it when it ran past him and through the hall under the stairs.

Susanna Wesley recorded, 'One night it made such a noise in the room over our head as if several people were walking; then running up and down stairs, and was so outrageous that we thought the children would be frightened so your father and I rose and went down in the dark to light a candle. Just as we came to the bedroom at the bottom of the broad stairs, having hold of each other, on my side there seemed as if somebody had emptied a bag of money at my feet, and on his as if all the bottles under the stairs (which were many) had been dashed to a thousand pieces. We passed through the hall into the kitchen, and got a candle and went to see the children.'

The following night, Susanna reported, there had been an independent witness, a Mr Hole (or Hoole) who was the rector from nearby Haxey, who had heard for himself the loud knocking at 2.00 a.m. with the elder Wesleys. That night the noise sounded like a carpenter planing deals, although on other occasions it sounded like the winding up of a jack. Often the entity would knock three times, then three times more, and so on for hours at a time.

Often the younger children would sleep through the nightly ordeal and there is some suggestion that they began to treat the manifestation – Old Jeffrey – as a friend. Apparently they would sometimes chase the knockings from room to room for fun. But for the older family members it was a disturbing, frightening time. One of them chronicled, 'it was beyond the power of any human creature to make such strange and various noises.' One of the maids had been so petrified after hearing an unearthly noise sounding like someone dying nearby that she refused to move from one room to another by herself.

The nightly appearances of the poltergeist were pre-empted by the strange behaviour of the household pet, a large mastiff that would start to act up suddenly, barking and leaping around at nothing. Gradually it would become more fearful before it would slink away, whining and trembling, to a hiding place under the stairs. Soon afterwards, the knocking and banging would begin.

Samuel Wesley.

Susanna Wesley.

One night, Samuel Wesley lost his patience with the entity. As knockings plagued one of his daughter's bedrooms he angrily drew his pistol and challenged the invisible menace to leave helpless children alone and face him 'man to man' in his study. The following night the normally peaceful study resounded to the poltergeist's knocking. It was becoming clear to Samuel that perhaps the poltergeist was an agent of evil, sent to test the family's faith – for what else could the phantom's appearance in the study mean but a mocking answer to his challenge? As he attempted to enter his study a powerful force is alleged to have pushed the door back in his face, but eventually he managed to battle his way into the room.

But at least the poltergeist had heeded his order to leave the children alone, so Samuel's next course was an attempt to communicate with the thing. He provided a number of raps on the wall and was answered by the same number and sequence of raps, as if by some invisible, mocking hand. Samuel, in his quest, followed the poltergeist into virtually every room in Epworth Rectory during the outbreak, and would often sit alone, door closed, and ask it what it wanted. Frighteningly, he never heard what he could discern as an articulate human voice – only two or three pathetic squeaks. The sign that the thing was in a room at any given time was the 'dead hollow note' which marked its presence.

It was now apparent that not only was the poltergeist becoming bolder, it was also becoming violent. Samuel recorded that on at least three occasions something unseen had forcefully shoved him, and furthermore the clergyman from Haxey – Mr Hole – was roughly shoved by the entity as he sat with Samuel one evening. And if the poltergeist was becoming more violent, it was also becoming stronger: on more than one occasion beds were seen to levitate themselves off the floor.

Friends and neighbours were by now becoming worried for the hounded family, but Samuel Wesley refused to be intimidated. 'Let the Devil flee from me; I will not flee from the Devil,' he told them.

At the end of January 1717, the outbursts that had plagued the Wesley's for two months stopped as suddenly as they had started. Emily records one last appearance by the poltergeist, writing in a letter dated 1 April 1717: 'The sprite was with us last night, and heard by many of our family.' It seems that Samuel Wesley's resolute defiance of the entity had won out, and this bears out what is known of the man. It is said that he had taken the family to Epworth after having to leave his previous parish because he took offence at the squire's mistress talking to his own wife, Susanna. Samuel Wesley, in fact, appears to have been somewhat hot-tempered and unpopular in Epworth, and there are those that claim that the 1709 blaze that gutted the rectory was in fact an arson attack on the parsonage. Similarly, there are those that think that the whole episode of Old Jeffrey was a hoax perpetrated by Samuel Wesley's political enemies in order to use his devotion to frighten him and his family from the parish.

This supposition notwithstanding, the family's written experiences were later collated by John Wesley, planting the seeds of a lifelong interest in the spiritual and the paranormal. There are those that point out that it is significant that although John collated his family's accounts there was one of his siblings who never chronicled her experiences – his sister Hetty. Over the years sceptics seeking to explain away the haunting at Epworth Rectory have pointed the finger of suspicion closer to home than any arsonist – they have blamed the nineteen-year-old Hetty for the disturbances.

On the face of it, it seems a trifle odd that Hetty was the only family member who did not write of her experiences: for judging by the writings of the others the poltergeist seemed to manifest itself around her more than anyone else. One of Hetty's sisters recorded: 'The noise never followed me as it did my sister Hetty. I have been with her when it has knocked under her and, when she moved, it has followed and still kept just under her feet.'

Hetty's mother, Susanna, wrote that on several occasions Hetty had been seen to shake and tremble in her sleep, and this always meant that the phantom noises were on their way; the knockings would wake the poor girl up. Susanna wrote: 'It was commonly nearer her than the rest.'

The closest thing to any kind of rational explanation for the Epworth haunting is that Hetty managed to set up a sophisticated and elaborate set of secret strings, pulleys and weights which she manipulated un-noticed, thus causing the strange knockings and other noises. A modern elaboration on this might suppose that at nineteen years old, Hetty may have been rebelling, or was even being manipulated by a sweetheart who represented one of Samuel Wesley's political opponents. When she was observed to tremble in her bed, she was in fact, stifling giggles because she knew that the 'spirit' was about to put in an appearance.

But the supposition that Hetty – even aided and abetted by a suitor – was behind the Epworth phenomena doesn't hold much weight. It would have to have been an extremely sophisticated system she used for the hoax to fool a household of family members and servants who were searching for an explanation. And such ropes and pulleys do not explain the invisible forces that shoved Samuel Wesley or the fact that the knockings sometimes emanated from the air in the *middle* of a room, much less the behaviour of the mastiff. Animals are notoriously perceptive of paranormal phenomena in cases such as this, and it has to be restated that the entity's appearance around Hetty was typical of their equally notorious attachment to young adults. It can be argued that perhaps the reason why Hetty was the only one who did not chronicle the events is because she was simply too traumatised by them. An individual is highly unlikely to have been behind the events at Epworth, and although a conspiracy of some sort involving half-a-dozen people is marginally more feasible it is still stretching the bounds of credibility that some evidence was not uncovered. One wonders why, if someone was that *desperate* to get rid of the Wesley's, they abandoned their efforts after only two months.

John Wesley compiled his family's experiences in 1720, speaking to each of those concerned and drawing on their written records. His account was published in three issues of *The Arminian Magazine*, and sixty years later it was repeated in the same periodical – the second time was during his lifetime, indicating that he was still as convinced of the manifestation as he had been in 1720. In his lifetime he wrote, 'With my latest breath will I bear witness against giving up to infidels one great proof of the invisible world, I mean that of witchcraft and apparitions, confirmed by the testimony of all ages.'

Although there is a clear religious message here of good triumphing over something evil, it must be pointed out that the trustworthy character of the witnesses is the key issue to the credibility of the Epworth case. And it should be noted that whilst the Wesley's were never again troubled by the poltergeist (although some accounts claim that daughter Emily, perhaps traumatised, was bedevilled throughout her adult life), more than a hundred years later Old Jeffrey is reported to have been behind similar activity at the rectory once again. In the mid-1800s, the then rector of Epworth was forced to leave the parsonage by the outbreak, and perhaps the entity still resides there.

The Binbrook Poltergeist

In January 1905 something evil visited Walk Farm, isolated high on the Lincolnshire Wolds near Binbrook. The farm was owned by William Drakes of Tealby, but was worked by the White family; solid, down-to-earth Lincolnshire folk, highly unlikely to fabricate any of the madness that was visited upon them. Local villagers spread sinister rumours about the place in hushed voices, but for the folk who lived and worked there the outbreak was very real and very frightening. Although some of the phenomena sounded too wild to be believed, there were always witnesses who would back up stories; and years after the events those witnesses still stuck to their accounts of their bizarre brush with the supernatural.

When the poltergeist materialized at Walk Farm, the first signs it had arrived were the typical types of behaviour associated with such an entity: objects were thrown around or mischievously hidden in other rooms. Some objects unaccountably toppled from level shelves. Potted plants tipped to one side then straightened themselves for the benefit of witnesses; brooms moved by themselves; and, bizarrely, it was claimed that a dead rabbit which hung on a hook outside had been seen to detach itself before running around the kitchen as though alive. Then it hurled itself back onto the hook and hung lifeless once more.

This last event, if true, indicates that what started out as a 'classic' poltergeist encounter was in fact rapidly revealing itself to be an altogether stranger phenomenon. This was borne out as the days went on and events began to turn more sinister.

Mrs White found that some of the chickens in the hen houses were being slaughtered and skinned during the night. As this went on, a guard was posted to keep watch for anyone creeping

An early twentieth century photograph of Binbrook's 'Bewitched Farm'.

up on the farm's property. But still the killings went on, violently and soundlessly in the night, and by the time it stopped some 226 birds had been killed – without any clue as to how it was happening. Watches had been mounted round the clock yet, as reported by the *Louth and North Lincolnshire News* of 28 January 1905, whenever the birds were checked on another four or five had been unaccountably slaughtered. All were killed in the same manner: 'The skin around the neck, from the head to the breast, had been pulled off, and the windpipe drawn from it's place and snapped.'

Following on from this was a terrifying scare involving a teenage servant girl. The girl was someone 'taken from the workhouse' to be employed as a servant. Mr White told the *Louth and North Lincolnshire News* of 28 January 1905 that the girl was sweeping the kitchen floor when, from the middle of the clothing on her back, smoke began to smoulder before flames erupted. Mr White walked into the kitchen and shouted in alarm at the flames bursting forth from the dress on her back, and at this she turned round and saw them for herself. In a panic she rushed through the door but tripped and fell over; Mr White managed to half fill some sacks with water and throw them over the poor girl, who was badly injured in the incident and needed to be taken to Louth Hospital. She had been nowhere near a small well-guarded fire at the other end of the kitchen when this happened, so this would appear to be a case of spontaneous human combustion; but the timing of the incident indicates that it was in some way linked to the entity that was plaguing Walk Farm. There is a disturbing suggestion that the fire had been burning the girl's back for some time as she swept, unaware of her danger. There is also some evidence that prior to this there had been unexplainable small fires breaking out at various places at Walk Farm.

Following this was another astonishing incident witnessed by many people working the land at the farm. One of the labourers had gone into a shed to hitch a pair of horses to a wagon. However, when he tried to move them off the horses did not move… and it was not for lack of trying. It was as though something massive and heavy – yet invisible – now lay in the wagon, preventing the straining team from going anywhere. Two more horses failed to make any difference, so the labourer attached two more; six horses in all, and still the wagon was too heavy for them to pull.

By this time a crowd of fascinated workers had gathered, and amongst the onlookers was Mr White, the farm tenant and foreman, who had perched himself in a wheelbarrow to get a better look. Suddenly, and with no one at the handles, the wheelbarrow took off, carrying the hapless Mr White across the yard in front of the astounded group. This was too much, and some of the labourers fled in fear.

Rumour swept the surrounding area: an old witch had long ago cast a spell on the land, some said. Others claimed that the devilry was down to the restless spirit of a young girl who had been murdered on the site and still lay buried there, forgotten and lost

As in the case of the Epworth poltergeist, the Binbrook outbreaks ended after two months as suddenly as they had begun. The incident was widely publicized in the contemporary newspapers and the case became something of a prototype for such future outbreaks the world over. Modern theory, leaving aside witchcraft and evil spirits, favoured the theory that some sort of latent psychic energy 'leaked out' of someone who was seriously disturbed at the farm and somehow transformed itself into destructive energy. But those who favoured the traditional poltergeist explanation have quickly pointed out that once again there is a young teenage girl on the premises (the badly burned servant girl) to whom these kinds of entities appear to attach themselves. Others favour the theory that there was a series of million-to-one coincidences involved, or that those involved – all of them – were outright liars. The truth is that the whole affair, if reliably recorded, remains a frightening, enigmatic example of some kind of vicious psychic force that is as yet unknown.

Haunted Houses

Think that you're safe from paranormal entities because you don't live in a manor house, a draughty abbey or a 300-year-old pub? You may not be…

When storm clouds gather overhead, and the county is lashed by extreme weather, such forces of nature can themselves be quite frightening. But on 28 August 1930, as the most violent electrical storm in memory raged, flashing lightning suddenly revealed a ghostly monk to the startled occupants of a house in Gainsborough.

Another property in Gainsborough, a big, multi-roomed terraced house, is also alleged to have been haunted. A fascinating story claims that in the 1930s, the couple who owned the house allowed the woman's brother to lodge with them for a few months. Something of a Bohemian, the brother apparently spent much time experimenting with his 'psychic ability', and when he moved out unexpectedly it appears he left behind some kind of latent psychic energy which hounded the family for years. The force resided in an upstairs bedroom and took the form of disturbing poltergeist activity. In the years after the Second World War the woman took to sleeping downstairs, too terrified to go to sleep upstairs on account of a face which would peer at her through the posts of the banisters. This story was passed down through the generations of a local family, and there are many gaps in the tale. The exact location of the house is not given in the account (submitted to the *Fortean Times* website), although it still stands and is currently occupied.

Mr Ted Barningham, his wife and family fled their Grimsby council house in Newton Grove in September 1967 after being terrorized for weeks by a sinister presence that finally revealed itself. The malicious presence was first blamed for turning the gas taps on at night, although the supernatural disturbances actually appeared to be concentrated in a bedroom and were so violent that the worried Mr Barningham had an electrical engineer install closed-circuit television in the room; whatever the camera picked up was relayed to a monitor screen downstairs. After several hours, those assembled downstairs – some six people – watched an image slowly appear on the monitor. Their blood ran cold as it gradually took the shape of a 'hideous' old man in what seemed to be the garb of a monk.

Whatever had been tormenting the Barningham family had materialised and was upstairs! A brave member of the party opted to rush upstairs and into the bedroom, but as he did so those downstairs watched the form fade away on the monitor. The engineer who had rigged up the apparatus could offer no technical explanation whatsoever for the incident, and for the Barningham family it was the last straw.

Nearer the present day, there is an area of Bunker's Hill, on the edge of Lincoln and heading east out of the city, which seems to be a positive hotbed of paranormal phenomena, with reports of all kinds coming from this area of fields and its quarry site. A resident of Bunkers Hill, whose house backed on to the fields, recalled how in the 1990s she had been entertaining one of her girlfriends one night when she suddenly became aware of curious lights that blinked and flashed just outside in the back garden. The young women had not closed the curtains, for the house did not back onto an estate – merely the aforementioned fields. At first the householder thought that her contact lenses were playing tricks on her eyes … until her friend, who did not wear contact lenses, commented on the strange little lights flashing in the back garden.

It was at this point that the two women noticed that the atmosphere in the house had become 'strange' – possibly with that same dream-like quality that accompanies many paranormal experiences. A CD player suddenly began to play the music backwards, much to the mounting tension of the girls. They switched the power off and then back on again which seemed to rectify the problem. However, it was at this point that the chilling sound of a baby crying further spooked the two women. Unnerving indeed, for the crying came not from another house, but from the very building they were in, under their own roof … and there were no children there.

On 4 October 2003, the Bassetlaw Ghost Research Group undertook an investigation at the home of a young family, whose eight-year-old son claimed to have an invisible friend who could run at speed all over the house, crawl up the bedroom walls and walk across the ceiling on all fours. Their house was a picturesque 200-year-old cottage in Market Rasen, and the team registered mysterious 'cold spots' during the first day of their investigation. But as they got underway events took a disturbing twist.

The parents encouraged the boy to talk about his chum, and he told them of a nasty little girl he had encountered who had shaken him roughly and banged his head on the wall. Following on from this his father was in the bathroom when he heard someone – a childish, little girl's voice – say his name. That night as he lay in bed with his partner, something took hold of him and roughly shook him, badly bruising his arm. Bedclothes were mysteriously ruffled, as though something invisible had jumped on them, and pictures on the wall were tipped.

The family moved out, but came back when the investigators moved in. During their stay, the Bassetlaw Ghost Research Group observed more cold spots, and one member had their face scratched badly by something unseen.

A medium had detected some three presences in the cottage and declared that one, a little boy, was trying to control the eight-year-old son of the house. The other two entities were a man and a girl, and all three appeared resentful of the occupants of the cottage.

The team's medium conducted a service to help the three spirits pass over to the other side, and this was apparently successful. Yet before they went, one of the spirits delivered what seems to have been a parting shot. As the team packed away after their all-night sitting, something unseen pushed an investigator down the stairs with an almighty shove, injuring him badly.

The cottage at Market Rasen is currently reported to be at peace once again.

An encounter in Eagle

Around 1998 a young man called Scott had a brief brush with the supernatural whilst visiting his aunt's house on the corner of Thorpe Lane and High Street, opposite the entrance to the church in Eagle. Scott explained that he glanced towards the kitchen door, and saw within the kitchen what he at first took to be a hung sheet billowing with movement. But this was no piece of laundry … as he looked closer the shape took on the form of what seemed to be a powerfully built man moving through the kitchen and past the doorway. The figure was shadowy and ill-defined, but definitely human.

One has to wonder whether there is any connection between this sighting and the ghost of an on-the-run murderer named Murray who is held to haunt the Eagle area. In life, legend says, Murray was an exceptionally vicious man: he is said to have been a seaman who mutinied against Sir Francis Drake in Elizabethan times. Once back in England he went on a murderous cross-country rampage, living rough and killing at will before meeting his fate at Eagle. His ghost is alleged to be equally brutal. Murray's ghastly spectre has been sighted on numerous occasions as far away as the banks of the River Witham, on the other side of Lincoln. In 1992 a couple motoring past North Scarle in the direction of Eagle beheld the disturbing sight of a strange bald-headed man brutally stamping on something - or someone - at the side of the road. As the car slowed, and the driver asked the man if everything was okay, the man turned to the car and screamed at it – prompting the driver to take off at speed. The witness reported that as he drove off he could still see the strange man stamping on the object in his rear-view mirror.

After recovering their nerves the couple turned around and drove back to the site. There was no sign of the man, nor of anything on the ground. This sighting has been linked to the others alleged to be of Murray's ghost. All in all, if it was the ghost of Charles Murray that Scott witnessed in his aunt's house that day, then perhaps it is a blessing that the encounter was mercifully brief.

CHAPTER FOUR

LIFE WITH THE SPIRITS

The White Hart Hotel, Lincoln

The White Hart Hotel stands in the annals of the supernatural as a classic example of a haunted building. Situated in Lincoln's historic Bailgate area, some of the bedrooms command spectacular views of the cathedral, which stands behind the hotel. The White Hart is drenched in history; the doomed King Richard II endowed it with it's emblem during a stay in 1372, when it was a coaching inn; the narrow corridors lead past rooms donned with plaques naming Lincoln's bishops that illustrate it's impressive heritage, for the building dates back to the 1400s (and may have its roots in an inn that stood there as far back as the late 1200s). Perhaps those tourists who choose to stay in this splendid area of Medieval Lincoln know of the rumours of haunted rooms. Perhaps they would rather not know.

Prior to its present incarnation, the White Hart had a notorious reputation as a den of thieves and vagabonds. One of these cutthroats still roams the hotel seeking revenge after his brutal killing sometime in the seventeenth century. One version of this event claims that a highwayman held up a coach near Lincoln, and the coachman managed to grab a fiery torch and ram it into the face of the bandit. The coach sped away towards the White Hart and left the horribly disfigured would-be robber writhing in his death throes on the ground. Another version claims that the soldiery were ordered to raid the inn, and during a pitched battle the highwayman was torched in the face as he tried to grab his sword in one of the rooms. Whatever the truth, the ghastly spectre of the highwayman has been spotted wandering the old coach yard: he holds up his cloak to hide his destroyed face, but witnesses claim that his eyes can still be seen – glaring with murderous intent as he apparently seeks those who killed him. On some occasions he has been glimpsed inside the hotel, with one account claiming he was spotted stumbling down a corridor with his disfigured face uncovered. His face was, it is said, as black as coal and his eyes were lifeless. It has even been claimed that he has been seen lying on the beds. Perhaps all sightings are of various stages of the highwayman's dying hours. A photograph taken in the Orangery is purported to show the ghost, but only from the chest downwards.

The highwayman is killed during a scuffle in one of the rooms at the White Hart.

Two centuries later, the area had prospered somewhat. But another ghost, known as the 'mob capped girl', illustrates that man's wickedness is never very far away. It is said that the girl was a maid who was strangled by the rat-catcher at the White Hart when she rebuffed his drunken advances. Centuries later she was reported as materializing in the landing on the stairs at the northeast corner of the building. The wretched spirit seems doomed to relive her last moments, for witnesses' report that she looks terrified and even cowers from them in a corner.

More recently in the apartments that overlook Bailgate, guests have been dumbfounded by the appearance of a figure dressed in a cravat and smoking jacket. This mysterious entity implores them to help him 'find my ginger jar'. He is possibly a former owner of the White Hart. Others claim that this smartly turned-out gent is an antiques dealer from decades ago who had one of his prize pieces – a ginger jar – robbed during a stay. They say that the shock killed the old gent, although perhaps he asked for it, because an add-on to this tale claims that he conned the ginger jar from an old woman who then cursed him. Apart from appearing to startled residents he is also blamed for the mysterious smell of cigar smoke that cannot be accounted for in the apartments.

In the 1960s, staff were amazed to witness a bizarre light which invaded the dining room. For some twenty minutes they watched a curious ball of light dance round the room, although this Will-o'-the-Wisp may not have been a ghost. Perhaps this mysterious ball of energy was the same thing that had apparently tormented a couple enjoying a meal some ten years previously. The outraged couple claimed that their romantic meal had been ruined by a force that threw all the cutlery off the table; the couple had persevered in true British fashion, even when the entire contents of a pepper pot had been dumped in the woman's soup. But when the man's steak jumped off the plate and landed in his lap they finally complained!

There is one particular room where the sense of sadness is almost overpowering. This is thought to be the room where a young man committed suicide in the early 1960s. Some fifteen years later, a visitor from Crowland asked the staff at reception what the small explosion he had heard in the middle of the night had been; no one could answer him, although some recalled that the suicide the previous decade had shot himself.

On the top floor a young man dressed in military garb from around 200 years ago has been clearly spotted.

However, the more recent phantoms seem centred around children. The young son of one of the owners of the White Hart would often talk about the strange, out-of-place lady he could see. When asked to describe her, he drew a picture of a figure in a long, flowing old-fashioned dress, and his ghostly 'nanny' had apparently even tucked him into bed once or twice. This was initially put down to the 'invisible friend' scenario that many children go through, but when the manager was awoken one evening by mysterious noises he found that a burning log had tumbled off the open fire and was smouldering on the carpet. He formed the opinion that the ghostly 'nanny' had awoken him deliberately to prevent a possible fire.

Two women staying in a room in the run-up to Christmas in the early 1990s complained that their sleep had been disturbed one evening by the sound of gleeful children playing noisily outside in the corridor. After much running, thumping and banging, the voices vanished into a

A view of the White Hart in Lincoln's historic Bailgate.

room at the end of the corridor, before returning to continue their playing. The following day the women informed staff that the children seemed to be a little boy and girl aged somewhere between eight and ten, and stated that they suspected they knew which room the children and their family were staying in. The two women were politely informed that the White Hart was rather quiet at that time of year, and there were certainly no families staying at that time; in fact the room from which the giggling and running sounds had emanated was most definitely empty. Given the hour and the number of staff on duty it was inconceivable that two little children had sneaked into the hotel to cause a rumpus. The event has remained an enigma.

In the lonely underground passages beneath the building, a sighting of a man in what seems to be the garb of a seventeenth-century cleric has been reported: it is thought that the passages lead directly to the cathedral in days gone by.

And in the quiet of the night some guests have heard phantom noises from outside – noises that appear to be columns of Roman soldiers marching, or centuries-old stagecoaches pulling up outside.

Finally, the author Jenny Bright discovered a story of a resident spectre at the White Hart that most people wouldn't even notice. A bedroom on the second floor is said to be the favourite dozing place of a ghostly tabby cat that trots up the corridor and *through* the bedroom door! One wonders how many staff members over the decades have shooed this animal away whilst cleaning the room.

It is quite an amazing catalogue of recorded incidents that the White Hart has amassed. And given that a significant number of reports would have come from tourists with no particular knowledge of the history of the White Hart Hotel, the evidence does indeed seem convincing that *something* is going on there … maybe one quiet night some unsuspecting tourist passing through Lincoln may just find himself sharing an entire hotel with the wraiths of those who have become attached to it's ancient floors and bedrooms!

The Angel and Royal Hotel, Grantham

Although the White Hart takes the prize for the greatest number of resident spooks (and indeed ranks as one of the most haunted buildings in the UK), it is far from the only place in Lincolnshire where you may find your evening disturbed by a paranormal entity.

The Angel and Royal Hotel in Grantham has an illustrious history. Originally built as a meeting place for the illustrious Brotherhood of the Knight's Templar, there stood an inn on the site for around 200 years before the façade of the current hotel sprung up in around 1400. The tyrannical King John stayed with his retinue in 1217, and King Richard III is reputed to have signed the Duke of Buckingham's execution order in 1483 whilst staying at the hotel.

But it is the poltergeist-like activities in a certain room that have disturbed visitors over the years. The disturbances may be linked to the wraith of the White Lady, whose spirit has been spotted moving along the second-floor corridors in the upper part of the hotel.

The White Lady has been spotted with fascinating frequency. In fact, she is seen so regularly that it is possible to provide a very good description of her. The ghost is of average height and slim in build; her hair is tied back in a plait or bun, and she wears a full length white or cream dress which has earned her the name. Reports of the dress itself are fascinating – it has a fitted bodice, and a very full skirt that appears stiff, rather than the usual flowing of a loose dress. This

The Angel and Royal Hotel, Grantham.

detail is interesting as it suggests the dress is of the sort that had a 'framework' to keep it in shape, and somehow this minor point adds a degree of authenticity to the reality of the White Lady.

An appearance by the White Lady in 1999 so terrified a guest that she fled her second-floor bedroom to spend the night with a friend who was in a room on another floor. In 2001 the manageress at the Angel and Royal Hotel was accosted by an American woman who wanted to know why she had not been told her bedroom was haunted: for she had awoken in the half-light of early morning to see a lady dressed in white standing at the end of her bed. The White Lady had stood and looked at the tourist for some seconds before turning and walking away, gradually vanishing as she did so.

The Vine Hotel, Skegness

The Vine Hotel in Skegness is said to be the haunt of Alfred, Lord Tennyson, who wrote *Maud* while he was living at the Vine Hotel in the 1850s. The poet died in 1892 but the phantom of an old man with a white beard walking down a corridor has been reported by staff, who have likened the ghost to pictures of Tennyson. The ghost has also been seen to be accompanied by two dogs.

A postcard image of Skegness Clock Tower and seafront in the early 1900s.

The Vine Hotel was for years said to be haunted by the ghost of a murdered customs officer. Locals said that in the seventeenth century an excise man had staged a lone raid on the Vine, and vanished in the nest of vipers that drank and plotted there in those days.

It is worth pointing out that in more violent days such communities existed. Coastal hamlets like Grainthorpe, Saltfleet and other marshland villages were hotbeds for smugglers, waiting for ships to crash at night on the rocks, before running to the beaches to raid whatever cargo drifted ashore from the unlucky vessel. Notorious smugglers like James Waite and Thomas Hewson – suspected in the robbery and murder of a young man in Sloothby – were active in Skegness.

One famous local tale tells how, in 1629, the people of nearby Burgh-le-Marsh attempted to stop the sexton, a man called Guymer, of St Peter and St Paul's church, from ringing the church bells to warn the *Mary Rose* of her dangerous proximity to the coast. The sexton had barricaded the church doors, and the angry mob outside swelled with murderous fury as the *Mary Rose* changed her course away from the shore. When the mob broke the door down, they found the old sexton dead from the effort of his heroism.

These tales provided a compelling reason for superstitious locals to beware areas where smuggling gangs operated. Strange lights on lonely cliff tops and beaches were avoided, as were dens of criminality, such as the Vine was reputed to be.

In the early twentieth century (one account claims 1902), workmen at the Vine demolishing part of a wall to put in a display cabinet uncovered the skeletal remains of the unfortunate customs man, bricked into the partition and still in his rotting clothes. This seemed to add credence to the old tale of the ghost, and further evidence that it was not merely a myth invented by coastal rogues. The room where the skeleton was discovered is now the Grill Room.

The ghostly customs man has been observed wandering along corridors and in and out of rooms. Upstairs in Room 8 guests have complained that a figure in a centuries old uniform has been seen standing by their bedside during the night. He vanishes before their eyes. And Room 8 is almost directly above the partition wall where the unfortunate customs man was bricked up.

Petwood Hotel, Woodall Spa

Petwood Hotel, at Woodhall Spa, was built around 100 years ago in thirty acres of Lincolnshire woodland, and boasts fifty-odd bedrooms. In 1943 it became the officer's mess for 617 squadron – the legendary Dam Busters, and a bar named The Squadron Bar commemorates this. It is not entirely surprising then that the shades of former airmen are alleged to wander the corridors. One visitor, Gordon West, claims that he sighted the spirit of the famous hero of the raids on the Ruhr dams, Wing Commander Guy Gibson. Gibson had been killed in action in September 1944 and his death is still something of an enigma; he may have died when his Mosquito crashed with engine failure at Steenbergen, Netherlands, or he may in fact have been shot down and killed, aged just twenty-five.

West thought he spotted Gibson walking towards the Lancaster Bar. He was smiling, and West recognised him instantly. However, it was not until he returned home that he realized the date was 19 September – the anniversary of Guy Gibson's death.

The sound of the Dam Busters team drinking has been heard when all is quiet, perhaps a phantom echo of a celebrated victory … or perhaps a final toast before they set off on another dangerous mission.

The Abbey Hotel, Crowland

For the tourist, there is little doubt as to the beauty of Crowland, a small town on Lincolnshire's extreme southern border with Cambridgeshire. A curious three-sided bridge, Trinity Bridge, dates to the fourteenth century and confirms that much of the area – before drainage – was marshland. Trinity Bridge now stands on dry land, but at one time traversed two rivers, long since diverted. But those who take the trip to see this unique piece of architecture will no doubt be struck by something else. There is a curious, isolated sensation about the town, possibly brought on by the journey there: as though it is strangely removed from the rest of Lincolnshire. Looking at the flat lands that surround Crowland, it is easy to envisage the old tale that turned up in the archives of the Huddleston family of Cambridgeshire: that of a traveller called Isaac Kirton, who stayed at a remote inn here in the early 1700s and was visited in the night by the ghosts of three drovers. The drovers had been murdered by the innkeeper, and the three spectres silently led Kirton to their graves so the crime would be discovered.

It is perhaps no surprise that only the stumbling footsteps of a ghost are heard at the Abbey Hotel in Crowland, just along the street from Trinity Bridge. For they are said to be those of Henry Girdlestone, a local farmer who drunkenly boasted in 1844 that he could walk 1,000 miles in 1,000 hours. Off he set on his marathon challenge, and by the time he staggered back into the Abbey Hotel he had covered some 1,025 miles – but in 1,176 hours. Perhaps his frustration at narrowly losing the bet is the reason why his footsteps are sometimes heard echoing from an attic.

The Abbey Hotel is also reputed to be home to the ghost of a woman who was murdered in one of the rooms. Little is known of this lady's fate, but in October 2002 manager Brian Berchielli claimed that several patrons had reported a ghostly little old lady with 'wispy grey hair' in the upstairs function room: perhaps she is the forgotten murder victim of long ago?

An early photograph of Crowland; the Abbey Hotel is just along the street from the famous three-sided bridge in the town centre.

The Great Lincolnshire Pub Crawl

Roughly seven miles northeast of Lincoln lies Welton, a charming village of around 4,500 residents. The Black Bull public house is perhaps Welton's most famous feature, visible as it is from the main road. But few of the drinkers who stop for a pint as they pass through know of its darker side. Owners of the place had often reported hearing footsteps on the stairs and the landing, yet when they rushed to challenge who they thought was an intruder, they found no one there. This same entity was blamed for objects being whisked off shelves in an upstairs kitchen. On a number of occasions the ghostly form of a Second World War airman has been spied; The Black Bull was near RAF Scampton, and during their time at Scampton, 617 Squadron – the Dam Busters – would travel to the pub for a drink. However, the airman was not the only suspect for the activity since others had reported two more ghostly forms dressed in clothing from the 1800s. A boy who has appeared at the pub is thought to be a stable-lad who died attempting to rescue horses from a burning stable in the grounds of the pub, and the ghost of a mill worker, who was fatally injured when he fell down some stairs, has also materialized.

In 1986, BBC Radio Lincolnshire conducted a psychic experiment at The Black Bull with a selected team of investigators, including a medium. During a night-time séance, the medium channelled a message from the spirit of the very airman whose presence would not leave the pub. He said his name was Paul Reed and he had been based at RAF Scampton during the war. He had been due to marry his sweetheart, but four months before the wedding he had been killed in action during a dogfight over the North Sea. During this event the airman was visible to the medium, whose description of him tallied with the other reports of the ghost: young, blonde hair, leather flying jacket, etc. The young flyer could not leave The Black Bull because of the many happy pre- and-post raid celebrations that he and his chums had shared there in life.

Three months later the landlord allowed the research party to return and conduct another séance. This time others saw and felt the presence of the young airman; and this time he was accompanied by a friend who identified himself as 'Phillip'. The two were spotted by some of those assembled sniggering conspiratorially together; the glass on the table that moved from one letter to the next eventually spelt out 'HA HA HA'. It seems the ghosts were playing tricks.

It is worth pointing out that this kind of haunting highlights the eternal dilemma of what 'ghosts' are, for if these events happened exactly and truthfully as described, then it is clear that the two airmen were capable of interaction with the living, whereas some hauntings – including many chronicled in these pages – indicate mere spectral re-enactments of some forgotten event.

The White Hart, Newton-on-Trent

On 27 October 2004, the *Lincolnshire Echo* carried a story about another haunted White Hart – this time a pub in High Street, Newton-on-Trent. When the landlords, Peter and Karen Taylor, took over the pub in 2001 they were tormented by moving tables, smashing glasses

SHADOWY SHAPES: The landlady of the White Hart pub in Newton-on-Trent, Karen Taylor, is menaced by a spectre in the bar. Picture: Ian Jubb. Picture reference: 4-6931-4.

Ghoulish glee of spook who spits on customers and breaks pub glasses

How the Lincolnshire Echo *reported the story of the Newton-on-Trent haunting.*

and – unusually – phantom 'spitting'. After four wine glasses flew off the wall rack, a team of mediums were called in.

A séance was held in a darkened room upstairs, with those assembled sitting round a table holding hands. In the gloom a bottle in the centre of the table began to move, and spelt out the name Zachary Arkwright. This unpleasant entity apparently took possession of the medium conducting the séance, for she began to speak in a gruff male voice, slammed her fists on the table, spat on those assembled, and growled, 'Why do you mock me?' The table then flew across the room and into the toilet, dragging those sat around the table with it. An attendee at the séance, Tracey Rowley, testified to the genuineness of the experience in the newspaper's article.

Once the group had gathered their nerves the séance began again. This time using the bottle on the table to answer the questions, Zachary Arkwright confessed that centuries before, on the site where the toilet block stood in the White Hart, he had murdered a young girl named Betsy because he thought she was a witch.

In what would seem to be an unrelated haunting, a child reported seeing a ghostly figure sitting in the corner of the bar. That was a mere two days before the *Lincolnshire Echo* article. It can only be wondered if the White Hart will produce yet more surprises in the future.

Woodcocks Inn, near Saxilby

Woodcocks Inn, at Burton Waters Marina near Saxilby, is another pub that has attracted the attention of ghost-hunters, in this case the Lincolnshire Paranormal Research Team. Landlord Don Osborn, aged thirty-eight, reported mysterious 'cold spots' in certain places in the pub, and claimed objects vanished. More disturbingly, he and his staff have seen shadows of spectres; and chillingly, on a number of occasions a man has been spotted outside walking up to the door, yet when staff open it to him he is nowhere to be seen. A thorough investigation in November 2004 was planned using infrared cameras, thermometers and motion-sensors, as well as holding a more traditional séance to rouse the spirits. The team interviewed staff members and were told of ill-defined, wispy figures that floated through walls, but although a drop in temperature was recorded in the corner of one room, and a séance was held, the results were inconclusive.

All in all, the Lincolnshire Paranormal Research Team has visited the place five times with various degrees of success. Curiously, on the first visit, one of the team suddenly reported being overcome by nausea. The sensation, he explained, was something akin to being given dentist's gas. This happened outside the gates to the building and it was later confirmed by the owner to be the spot where some years previously a man had committed suicide by gassing himself to death in his car. Apparitions have also been reported inside the building, and strange voices have been heard.

The Centurian, North Hykeham

At the Centurian pub in North Hykeham, a man having a drink with his father in 2004 was greatly disturbed to see a spirit. He glanced in the direction of an archway and saw what looked like a lady in a long nightdress, her hair curled under in the fashion of one who is about to go abed. He glanced away, taking his eyes off the woman for only a second; yet when he looked back she had vanished, with nowhere she could have gone or hidden.

The Homestead, Bracebridge Heath

In 2004, a family meal at the Homestead in Bracebridge Heath was interrupted by the four-and-a-half year-old grandson repeatedly claiming that a sinister-looking man by a wooden and glass partition was looking at him. The other family members could not see anyone at all, but the child would not eat and became agitated and frightened by this unseen figure. As they left, the child looked fearfully at the spot where the thing was. The family were adamant that the child was incapable of lying about such matters and had never done so before, and it appears that other patrons may have sensed a presence at the Homestead.

It is interesting to note that in a former life the Homestead was part of the old St John's Hospital, which was closed down in 1989. St John's had itself once been the Lincolnshire County Lunatic Asylum. Local stories tell that a grey lady walks through one of the rooms in what is now the Homestead, and comes to a halt in front of the fireplace. It is also reported that a ghostly man in a thick coat can be seen sitting at one of the tables near the bar. Perhaps this is the sinister figure that frightened the young boy so much in 2004.

In 2005 there came confirmation that the Homestead had been haunted for years. After reading the above experiences on the BBC website, 'Gareth' contacted the site to relate his own experiences at the pub. A few years ago he had known the landlord and landlady of the

The Homestead in Bracebridge Heath. In overgrown scrubland behind the pub there can be found the deserted ruins of the old lunatic asylum.

Homestead – and they had been forced to leave because of the ghostly goings on. Gareth confirmed that he had witnessed some phenomena for himself when he had been invited by the couple to the Homestead. He saw beer taps in the cellar turn themselves on: when they were turned off, they were later found to have somehow been turned *on* again.

But the landlord and his wife experienced much more than this. In the office upstairs, the sound of something heavy being dragged across the floor was heard. But on investigation nothing was found to have been moved, nor anything heavy enough to have made the frightening noises.

Loud bumps emanating from the top of the stairs were also found to have no cause. A little digging into the Homestead's former life as an asylum suggested that an inmate had hanged themselves at the top of the staircase – and the mysterious noises sounded like nothing so much as swinging feet bumping and kicking the banister. (NB: This incident is all the more unnerving for another reason. The four-and-a-half year old grandson whose sighting prompted the focus upon the Homestead had made a bizarre remark after he 'saw' the man in the thick coat in 2004. In the car on the way home the unnerved child had made a cryptic comment about 'string, but thicker and hanging'.)

The couple put up with the activity for some months but one evening the final straw came. The woman awoke in the middle of the night and instantly froze with fear at the sight of a dark figure lurking in the corner of the bedroom. She then sensed that there was another figure closer at hand, immediately at her side. She turned her head to find a lady dressed in white, who took her hand and stroked it, and reassured the landlady that she should not be scared.

Perhaps the landlady had an otherworldly encounter with a nurse and a distressed inmate? Whatever the reason, Gareth reported that after this uncanny event his friends upped and left the Homestead to run another pub some way away. Apparently, all who owned the Homestead had at some time or another experienced similar phenomena.

Maybe it is only natural that the Homestead is the focus of rumours and stories, given its background. Ever since the first reports of something strange at the Homestead, reports of incidents there have accelerated. The place appears to have been somewhat unknown in paranormal circles until recently, but it is increasingly apparent that it has quite a supernatural history and warrants monitoring.

Lincoln's Haunted Pubs

From the Lord Nelson, Brigg, in the north, where two members of staff reported that a customer sitting in the corner at the bar simply vanished, to Stamford in the south, where the Black Bull in Stamford Walk has a phantom carriage that allegedly sweeps through the old carriageway, there are literally scores of haunted pubs throughout Lincolnshire. But it is the city of Lincoln itself that boasts the finest collection of haunted drinking establishments.

In September 2004, the *Lincolnshire Echo* ran a competition for its readers: the writer of the most believable true ghost anecdote would win a chance to join Project Ghost Hunt in an investigation at The Lawn. Nowadays, The Lawn is a bar with an impressive open-plan back 'garden' commanding a good view of the city: the ideal venue for a wedding party or the like. But 170 years ago it was opened as one of the first mental hospitals in Britain, and stories have persisted that the tortured spectres of disturbed patients still wander the building, wailing in vain.

The historic Lion and Snake in Lincoln's Bailgate, c. 1900.

The Lion and Snake public house stands in Bailgate on the direct route of the old Roman road through Lincoln and may well be the oldest inn in the city, dating as it does from the 1400s. Given this, it is no surprise that it hosts several resident spooks. It is rumoured that a Roman soldier haunts the cellar, but its best-documented phantom is that of a mysterious old woman described as a typical granny: grey hair tied in a bun, stooped over and in her mid-seventies. In the 1980s a relief landlord had an embarrassing moment when he left the bathroom one afternoon, clad in a towel ... and bumped into the strange old woman in the corridor. He even pressed his back to the wall of the narrow corridor to allow her to pass him! When he questioned the regular landlord and lady downstairs in the private lounge he was dumbfounded. For they told him that in all probability he had just witnessed the resident ghost, whom they had themselves bumped into on several occasions. The old woman had looked totally 'real' to the witness – but she had not been of this earth.

But downstairs, where the public gather and enjoy a beer, another spirit has been spotted. If you should be drinking towards the rear of the bar, you may chance to spot a rather unkempt, scruffy looking man who approaches the rear wall ... and vanishes into it. It is unknown who this figure is, but he was seen several times in the early 1990s – and the spot where he disappears used to be a kitchen doorway before being bricked up...

The Cornhill Vaults

The Cornhill Vaults witnessed a strange case of the 'phantom customer' phenomenon – more strange in that the ghost was of a modern-day young man. As its name would suggest, The Cornhill Vaults is underground in Lincoln's bustling city centre shopping district, and access is gained by a thin staircase and along a corridor. A staff member reported seeing the young man approach the bar, just as she turned away from it to head towards the kitchen: he was wearing a collarless shirt, unbuttoned at the neck. However, another staff member who was asked to serve the young man found no one there, and the only other person at the bar – another woman – denied that anyone else had approached. But the patron at the bar did say that some unaccountable feeling had made her blood turn to ice, as if someone had 'walked over her grave'.

The Jolly Brewer

The ghost that allegedly haunts the Jolly Brewer, in Lincoln's Broadgate, is heard but not seen. It is a bizarre haunting, one that takes the form of a voice who calls the names of the staff working behind the bar. The voice never bothers the customers, and somehow manages to make itself heard to the bar staff even through the noise of the drinkers or, more impressively, over the din of local bands that may be performing at the pub. In an interview with the *Lincolnshire Echo,* published on 1 April 2005, landlady Emma Chapman claimed that she had heard the invisible entity calling her name through the hubbub of the crowd. Indeed, most of the eight staff had at some time heard their names being called by something as they poured drinks for the customers. Those who have heard it are unable to ascertain whether it is a male or female voice who calls them, and can only describe it as 'a voice'.

The Witch and Wardrobe

At the Witch and Wardrobe, which faces out onto the River Witham in Lincoln's city centre, bar staff have reported pumps mysteriously turning themselves on and ice being thrown around by an invisible force.

The Green Dragon

Finally, our haunted pub crawl takes us to The Green Dragon, which stands at Waterside North on the edge of Lincoln's shopping district, next to the River Witham, the canal of which snakes through the city centre. The original building dates back to the fourteenth century and the age of the place can be felt in its distinctive Tudor-style exterior and four-pointed roof. In July 1994, the pub came under new management, and the new landlord found he had inherited a place with a resident ghost – that of a small old woman in a striped grey shawl who was spotted very clearly smoking an old-fashioned clay pipe. A barmaid had witnessed this apparition in the function room and on the top floor, and it had scared her so badly that she had resigned.

During the course of a routine conversation with an elderly lady who had lived in the building some fifty years before, it turned out that the diminutive ghost may have been the woman's grandmother, one Mary Cooper, who had kept an umbrella shop in the building which The Green Dragon now inhabited.

Over the next few months the new landlord himself experienced the supernatural mischief that this entity performed. The eerie incidents began, appropriately enough, on Halloween, when a ghostly party was heard coming from a locked room after hours; the landlord had himself only just previously locked the room up. The noises of the paranormal party faded away at midnight. Bottles being found unaccountably broken in the cellar followed this, and noises like beer kegs being dragged would reach the ears of staff sat assembled on the ground floor. Whilst serving customers, the gas taps that powered the beer pumping up into the bar were all simultaneously turned off, much to the annoyance of bar staff. But the taps were in the cellar, and it had been securely locked.

Upstairs, in the function room, chairs would be moved when staff preparing the venue left the room briefly, and on one occasion the entity apparently scattered a table-full of leaflets all around the room. During an investigation by the author and psychic Jenny Bright, whose account appears in *Ghosts of Lincoln*, the spirit of Mary Cooper 'told' her that she had turned off the gas taps as a Luddite-style protest at new machinery; the poor woman did not seem to realise that she had died.

After the psychic's visit, the noises from the cellar grew in intensity, and – bizarrely – a long kitchen knife was snapped in two by an unseen force, the two pieces being crossed and laid in an 'X' shape next to the joint of beef!

The snapped knife is now displayed on a wall in the Witham Suite, and so is a photograph of Mary Cooper procured from her granddaughter.

Strange things at the Black Horse

In Eastgate, in the shadow of Lincoln Cathedral, stands a twelfth-century building which has been a tavern of some kind for centuries, but in its current incarnation is the Black Horse Chambers Bistro and Bar. Further down Eastgate, on the cathedral side, a strange little stone creature is stuck high on a wall bordering the Minster Close. The creature is a gargoyle, and he looks to his left … directly at the Black Horse.

It is said that the inn was regularly filled with drunken clergymen in the sixteenth and seventeenth centuries, so the Bishop of Lincoln ordered the gargoyle be mounted on the wall to remind his clerics that God, and he himself, would always be watching them.

The Black Horse is said to be haunted by the shade of a lady in a long dress, who floats around the upstairs rooms. It is presumably the same spirit that a *Lincolnshire Echo* reader once spotted; she submitted a letter to the newspaper claiming to have seen a lady in Victorian clothing walk past an archway at the side of the Black Horse. The lady's face was 'blurry', and the witness likened it to an image one might see on an old photograph. In the 1980s a cleaning lady is held to have fled in terror after seeing the 'Grey Lady'.

It has been claimed that at one time the pub had literally scores of ghosts, so many that an exorcist had to be called in to get rid of them all.

In the mid-1990s an altogether different paranormal entity manifested itself at the Black Horse. The incidents began in the summer of 1994 when the pub was undergoing a complete refurbishment, including structural alterations, redecorating and rewiring. The force that appeared at this time appears to be distinct from the Grey Lady, and may have been some kind of latent psychic energy unleashed by the disturbances of the renovation. The phenomena began with typical poltergeist activity, which continued to plague the place on-and-off during the renovations and after the Black Horse had reopened for business.

In fact the closest thing to a physical presence the poltergeist might have had was accidentally 'released' late one autumn night in 1995 by two staff members. The evening had been very busy, and after the last drinkers had drifted off, the two members of staff remained behind chatting and decided to light the open log fire. The night was cold so they decided to put a little more wood on the fire.

The Eastgate gargoyle, looking out on the Black Horse.

At this, the fire flashed and roared dangerously into life, as though some kind of flammable liquid had been poured onto it. Above the noise of the intense flames, came an eerie low howling sound, like wind, emanating from the chimney above the fireplace. According to the two witnesses, it seemed to come down the chimney and into the room, where it swirled around them, leaving a chill in its wake. It appeared to move across the room, still faintly howling, towards the stairs; then it drifted up the stairs and along the upper floor of the building. The already frightened staff members jumped out of their skin when they heard a door bang shut somewhere nearby. At this everything went silent, and although the fire still burnt strongly, the room was left ice cold.

Both witnesses agree that it had not been an ordinary wind that had entered the room, more some sort of psychic force or entity.

CHAPTER FIVE

THE GHOSTS OF WAR

The RAF Cranwell Ghost Photograph

The photograph taken in 1919 on the runway of the airbase at Cranwell is one of the rare, impressive and downright spooky pictures that can actually claim to show a 'real' ghost.

The post-First World War group photograph was taken of the members of the Maintenance Group of HMS *Daedalus* and shows the men dutifully proud in their uniforms in six rows: the front row sitting, legs crossed, and each successive row behind stood at a slightly higher level so all can be seen. The sixth row, at the back, shows the face of mechanic Freddy Jackson, just behind the left shoulder of a uniformed flyer. The problem is that Jackson had been killed a few days earlier in a horrific accident on the runway, when he had tripped and fallen into the whirring blades of a propeller on an aircraft preparing to take off.

It has been put forward that the face peeping from behind the RAF man in the photograph is nothing but a splodge or blemish of some kind, but most of the photograph is very clear. The RAF man whom 'Jackson' is stood behind is in focus. Furthermore, if the face is a blemish, it is an exceptionally detailed one, very lifelike and with apparently a smile for the camera. And yet, the face is somehow opaque, faded, as though merely the shade of a human being.

The mysterious photograph first turned up in 1975, the background story being recounted in a book by retired Air Marshall Sir Victor Goddard entitled *Flight Towards Reality*. He had kept the image for many years after it had been taken down from the squadron bulletin board. 'Jackson's ghost', he wrote, 'appeared to be saying, "I nearly failed to make it! They didn't wait or leave a place for me, the blighters!"'

The apparent sombre expressions of the other men in the photograph are perhaps explained by the allegation that they had just returned from Jackson's funeral…

The photograph then appears to have ended up in the possession of Bobbie Capel, the widow of Air Vice Marshall Arthur Capel. In 1996, her neighbours in the village of Chipstable, Somerset, persuaded her to send the photograph to the *Navy News*, and the ninety-seven-year-old Ms Capel obliged. Thus it again came to public attention, nearly twenty years after

The RAF Cranwell ghost photograph.

its first mention in *Flight Towards Reality*, and a full seventy-seven years after it was taken by Bassano's Photographic Co. on the Cranwell runway. Ms Capel was adamant that the figure *is* that of Freddie Jackson, and that the negatives were studied at the time – and found to show no evidence of tampering. Bassano's were a professional photographic concern and no-one would have dared to tamper with the image, Ms Capel asserted. Furthermore, the photographer came from outside the base, knew no-one, including Freddy Jackson, and left straight after taking the photograph.

If all this is correct, then it leaves only one supposition: that the face in the photograph is, indeed, that of a ghost.

The Metheringham Phantom

The Metheringham Lass is one of the better-documented cases of haunting in Lincolnshire, somewhat in the theme of the classic 'phantom hitchhiker'.

Eight miles southeast of Lincoln, along the B1189 stretch of road, in the vicinity of RAF Metheringham, usually between the hours of 9.30 p.m. and 10.00 p.m., motorists, cyclists and even pedestrians have been stopped by a young woman in distress.

The description of the woman is unusually specific. She is in her late teens and reportedly very attractive, and she is wrapped up against the cold of the night in a pale green coat that has an RAF wings badge pinned to the lapel. Her reddish-brown hair is partly covered by a grey (or light blue) headscarf, and all those who have witnessed her say that she seems to be quite solid and 'real'.

She is also convincingly lucid. Those who pull over to help the young woman are told that there has been an accident. The woman tells them that she was riding on the pillion of her boyfriend's Royal Enfield motorcycle, when, on the wet road, he skidded and lost control. She was unhurt in the crash, but she has left her boyfriend injured and come along the stretch of road looking for someone to help her. The witnesses are often struck by a lavender fragrance.

Those Good Samaritans who have ventured along the road in the dark have reported that as they make their way towards the crash site the atmosphere becomes somewhat unreal, and fear and panic sets in. At the point of the crash site, nothing is found and the girl inexplicably vanishes in the darkness – the smell of lavender being replaced by the stench of decomposing flesh. In an encounter towards the end of the Second World War, one witness claimed that when he saw the young woman he found himself looking into a ghastly face that had no eyes, merely empty, skull-like sockets.

The ghost is thought to be that of nineteen-year-old Catherine Bystock, from Horncastle, who was engaged to an RAF aircrew Flight Sergeant stationed at RAF Metheringham. One night, as they roared in the direction of Metheringham village on his motorcycle after a dance, the Flight Sergeant lost control and they crashed near the point where the Metheringham Lass appears.

But it was not he who was killed; it was his young fiancée, Catherine, who died in the accident after being thrown from the motorcycle.

And now, it seems she is destined to relive her torment as unsuspecting motorists make their way past the abandoned remains of RAF Metheringham on dark, lonely nights.

The Ghosts of War: RAF Wickenby

Given the ferocious activity, trauma and triumph surrounding the county's many RAF bases during the Second World War, it would be remarkable if there were no hauntings associated with them. It is also noteworthy that such alleged hauntings provide a wealth of evidence that spectres are not merely confined to Roman soldiers, ancient murder victims and Cavaliers, but also something more tangible, nearer to our own time.

In his autobiography, the late comedian and founding member of the Goons, Michael Bentine, recalled a strange incident when he was stationed at RAF Wickenby in his position as RAF intelligence officer. One night after a week's leave in London, Bentine was walking to his quarters across the base after a heavy snowfall. In the moonlight he saw the tall figure of his friend – whom he referred to as 'Pop' in his autobiography – approaching him. The unmistakable frame of Pop was clearly illuminated by moonlight on the snowfall. 'Hi Pop, I've had a great leave', Bentine called to his friend in greeting – and saw the other man nod in acknowledgement and wave his hand. Bentine then entered his hut, last seeing Pop heading towards his own hut. It was just after midnight.

Some six hours later, upon being woken by his batman, Bentine learned during the course of routine conversation that his friend Pop had in actual fact been killed *two days previously* when a Lancaster he had opted to navigate on had crashed in the Lincolnshire Wolds during a night exercise. Everyone on board had died.

Since then, RAF Wickenby has earned the reputation of being so haunted it is almost as if the place is still operating as a Second World War airbase! Shades of figures have been glimpsed walking near the runway, and the ghosts of airmen have been seen smoking cigarettes … before vanishing from sight. At the control room, a pilot walks in before vanishing upstairs, and at the spot where the hangers used to be mechanics have been seen running as though on full red alert before disappearing. Ghostly whistling of old songs has also been heard. The ghost of a WAAF has also been reported – she is thought to be the spectre of a woman who killed herself at the site after learning that her fiancé had died during a mission, his aircraft raked by German gunfire. Most disturbing of all is the so-called headless cyclist. He is said to be the apparition of an unfortunate man who was decapitated on his bicycle by the propellers of an aircraft making manoeuvres on the runway.

These days, Lincolnshire Aviation uses Wickenby airfield for civilian flying training and have their offices in the old watchtower. A small museum has been set up in the watch office, where a display commemorates the heroism of 12 and 626 Squadrons. But the place is still alive with the presence of spirits, and to this day footsteps on the stairs and the sound of doors opening upstairs are reported. Upon investigation, of course, no one is found.

RAF Kirton-in-Lindsey

During 1940 and 1941, RAF Kirton-in-Lindsey came under bombardment during a Luftwaffe raid. Three years later, in 1944, LAC Hewitt was posted to the base, and in August of that year this young man suffered an unnerving experience. One night he was shaken awake by a terrified roommate who claimed he could hear bizarre screaming noises. The pair strained their ears and, sure enough, the young LAC tuned into what he thought were the sounds of screams and strange hysterical voices that sounded akin to the French language. The two searched unsuccessfully with torches for the source of the noises.

The following day, Hewitt was told about the raids on the base three years previously. One bombardment had destroyed Block 37, and killed many Free French pilots in the barracks. The RAF vacated the base in 1965, since when more screams have been heard, and a ghostly pilot has been spotted near a hangar.

RAF Binbrook

Prior to being abandoned in 1988, RAF Binbrook was, it appears, the earthbound home of a spirit who waved frantically and signalled at approaching aircraft … although the skies above remained clear. This mysterious airman has been reported on numerous occasions and is thought to be the ghost of an armourer, a sergeant who saw off a Lancaster as it took to the air on a mission during the Second World War. When the Sergeant realised that the aircraft had been accidentally loaded with armed bombs he chased after the Lancaster as it lumbered airborne. Too late, the unstable cargo detonated and took the aircraft with it in a fiery explosion. All on board died, and the sergeant on the ground – helplessly signalling the doomed craft – was also killed in the fallout from the blast. The distressed airman, who was reported by witnesses to be waving at nothing on the runway, is thought to be the ghost of the unfortunate sergeant. One source gives the tortured spectre the name of Sergeant Sinclair.

For years after the Second World War ended it was reported that an ethereal figure could be spotted walking the perimeter road outside RAF Binbrook. This spectre is alleged to be that of an Australian worker or airman at the base nicknamed 'Clubfoot' who died in an explosion whilst trying to sabotage a Lancaster bomber during the war.

RAF Digby

RAF Digby is one of the few RAF bases that remained active in Lincolnshire after the Second World War, becoming home to a number of training units in the 1950s and '60s. A mysterious officer wheeling his bicycle has, on numerous occasions, stopped airmen at the base and asked them to fetch the keys to the control tower. However, after the keys have been brought for him, he is nowhere to be found. Could he be the same manifestation that haunts the control tower itself, where unaccountable voices have been heard and lights were reported to be on during power cuts? In the 1950s, mysterious footsteps in an empty barrack block were reported by two airmen, and in the same block an off-duty airman awoke to see another airman – dressed in wartime garb – walk up to a bed and sit down on it, ready to relax. This figure then simply vanished when he was approached.

RAF Waltham

In North East Lincolnshire, the long-abandoned RAF Waltham, Grimsby, could be a ghost-hunter's dream. Following its desertion in 1945, one of the hangars was used by a local concern for storing grain and conveyor equipment. One evening, a shift worker tending to grain sacks was found running in terror through the hangar, and when his fellow workmen managed to bring him under control he blurted out an incredible tale. A phantom airman had, he claimed, suddenly walked *through* the hangar wall and into the ante-room, paused for a moment in front of the startled workman, and then walked through the opposite hangar wall. The spectre had been headless.

It is said that the incident so shocked the worker that he became a gibbering wreck and his hair came out in clumps. The ghost was thought to be that of a Lancaster bomber pilot who lost his life in a crash.

As if this wasn't enough, a local woman reported that in 1969 she had awoken in the middle of the night to find a ginger-haired airman – his uniform's empty sleeve clearly indicating that he had only one arm – standing at the end of her bed. The intruder looked at her and then turned away, before vanishing into a wardrobe. The house in which this incident happened was a mere two-years-old, and the street – Cheapside Road – had been built on the perimeter of RAF Waltham, near some of the concrete bases on which the old huts had stood. During the Second World War, the huts had been ripped by a blast, possibly by a suicidal airman who had been refused permission to fly because his battle injuries had made him unfit to do so.

More serene is the spectre who was reported a number of times in the early 1980s, apparently paying silent tribute to fallen comrades. A ghostly airman was said to appear in his flying kit at the memorial to No. 100 Squadron in a lay-by off the A16, which crosses one of RAF Waltham's old runways.

RAF Fiskerton

It must have been a disturbing day at RAF Fiskerton for the secretary who was rudely ignored by a mysterious airman in full RAF garb when she addressed him. During the Second World War, the woman had been attending to her duties in the control room, a highly secure underground part of the complex. Upon returning to her office above ground, she reported her encounter to her Deputy Group Commandant. The two were, at the time, the only people on the premises, and moreover, the only people with access to the control room. Who had the silent airman the secretary had seen walking away down an underground corridor been? And how had he managed to infiltrate the secure complex?

The incident could be passed off as 'one of those things' were it not for the reports of ghostly voices in the old control tower in the years that followed the end of the war. And in the 1970s there was a strange encounter on the (by this time) desolate airbase, when a motorist taking lessons there was shocked by a phantom jeep, full of airmen, which sped past him, before disappearing out of sight around some boulders … and vanished.

This striking memorial stands by the runway of what was once RAF Fiskerton.

The RAF Skellingthorpe war memorial. The base itself no longer exists: the site is now the vast Birchwood housing estate.

RAF Skellingthorpe

In 1970, a woman who had spent her war years at RAF Skellingthorpe as a WAAF, returned for a nostalgic visit long after the base had closed in the early 1950s – and reported encountering the ghost of the man she had briefly been engaged to during her service at the base. He was walking along the perimeter tracks, yet he did not respond when she called out to him.

Furthermore, whilst looking at the control tower, the scene about her began to change. The sound of Merlin engines droned overhead, mechanics were suddenly running about and a Lancaster bomber was being kitted out. The woman noticed that an airman sat atop the bomb carrier of the Lancaster. Suddenly the scene changed again and she found herself looking at a sombre funeral and formed the impression that the poor man she had just seen had died when the bomb carrier he was sat upon blew up. Suddenly, at the click of a finger, she was back in reality and her friends were about her.

It is possible the woman entered a 'time-slip' – since it is by no means certain that her ex-fiancée of all those years ago was actually dead. RAF Skellingthorpe gradually turned into the sprawling Birchwood housing estate.

A Lancaster bomber and RAF personnel at Elsham Wold during the height of wartime activity.

RAF Spittlegate

When the RAF finally left RAF Spittlegate, near Grantham, in 1975 after nearly sixty years of service, the army moved in and replaced them. This, it seems, disturbed a spirit who switched lights on and off, and made candles jump from their holders. As the activity gained momentum, marching feet were heard – as well as the sound of long-departed aircraft engines. Two senior officers reportedly saw the entity – which appeared as a shadow-like figure in their room. The spirit was alleged to be that of Joe 'Tiny' Harris, who fulfilled various positions at RAF Spittlegate during the Second World War, including telephone operator. Perhaps the dedicated aircraftman could not bear the thought of his beloved Royal Air Force leaving the place.

RAF Elsham Wold

RAF Elsham Wold opened in 1941 in North Lincolnshire, and was a bleak outpost noted for its equally bleak weather – seemingly dusted with a perpetual covering of snow. In 1945, a WAAF reported stopping her car in thick fog after becoming lost in atrocious conditions out on the airfield. She thought her saviours had arrived in the form of three airmen in full flying gear who appeared out of the mist – but the men ignored her plea for help and vanished back into the fog. Also, there would have been no aircraft flying in such poor conditions.

The airbase ceased activity in 1947. In the years that followed a family of seven, the Gregorys', took up residence in the old control tower at Elsham Wold. Yet they shared their new residence with phantoms which tapped out Morse code messages on invisible machines.

On occasions the Gregorys were fortunate enough to spot their ghostly lodgers – spectral airmen who walked through walls or appeared at the foot of the bed; on one such occasion, a flyer was encountered sitting in a bedroom chair smiling at a thoroughly startled Mr Gregory! On each occasion the ghosts vanished in front of the witness.

One evening Mrs Gregory was brought running to the bedroom of her young son, Paul, who was screaming and trembling. 'Can't you hear that plane?' the distressed boy shouted. 'It's taking off and it's not coming back!' Paul went on to describe a large four-engine aircraft and it's seven man crew that he had seen alight from the disused runway; the craft bore the code letters 'PM'. Paul had seen the aircraft take off in the middle of the night from his vantage point in his bedroom (the converted old control tower, less than 100 yards from the abandoned runway).

He had then experienced his premonition that the ghostly plane would not return from its mission.

The *Grimsby Evening Telegraph* covered the Gregory's claims in 1976. The control tower at the centre of the haunting has since been demolished.

RAF Hemswell

A different kind of noise plagues RAF Hemswell, one of the county's oldest bases, which dates back to the First World War. In 1978, long after the site had been vacated and abandoned to the elements, a motorist reported that upon stopping to answer nature's call – the place was suitably isolated – his attention was drawn across the road to the premises of the old airfield. The music of a dance band sounded in the air, and the motorist recognised the tune as that of the *Missouri Waltz*. Further noises of an RAF base in full working order followed, including aeroplane engines starting, voices and the crunching of feet on the ground. The frightened man strained his eyes in the darkness but could see no signs of life at all. The only *actual* thing he saw was a flash of bright lights that accompanied the sound of a heavy truck not too far from him. The man got back into his car when the ghostly noises sounded as though they were moving closer towards him.

It seems a malevolent spirit also plagues RAF Hemswell. People have reported being pushed violently by an unseen perpetrator. One witness received his shove when he cried in alarm at the sight of a strange glowing airman in full flying gear. Perhaps there is a link between these incidents and the alleged sightings of the spectre of an airman running along the runway on fire, following the crash of his bomber...

Even gorier is the apparition of an engineer, who staggers around after losing an arm in some machinery, his screams echoing around the old airbase.

RAF East Kirkby has been saved from ruination, unlike many other airbases.

RAF Coleby Grange control tower, left to the elements … and haunted.

RAF East Kirkby

Like the previously mentioned RAF Hemswell, many deserted bases have fallen into disrepair. An exception is RAF East Kirkby, which has been saved from this fate by Fred and Harold Panton, who wanted the base kept alive as a tribute to their brother Christopher – who was stationed in North Yorkshire and who died on a raid on Nuremburg. RAF East Kirkby is now home to the Aviation Heritage Centre and boasts a reconstruction of a Second World War air traffic control tower – and a Lancaster bomber that taxis on the remains of the base's runway.

The Panton brothers have been aware of a supernatural presence in the tower, and visitors too have heard strange footsteps and other noises, as well as seeing inexplicable lights. Most disturbing of all is the heart-stopping sight of a young airman who has been spotted approaching the control tower. He is reported to be wearing the garb of a US Air Force airman; he half carries and half drags an open, burned parachute behind him. It is thought that he may be the ghost of a crew member (possibly the pilot) of a B-17 Flying Fortress, *Belle of Liberty*, which was denied permission to land at RAF East Kirkby in the chaotic period when other bombers were preparing to take off on raids. The *Belle of Liberty*, returning from it's own heroic raid, was attempting to make an emergency landing at East Kirkby, but was forced to circle until finally it crashed nearby, killing everyone on board.

In 1983, a visitor to the base watched as two men in US Air Force-type clothing walked towards the control tower, and entered the building. The witness then watched as two more men walked towards the building. Taking a closer look, his blood ran cold. The faces of the men were white with the pallor of death. Were they the spirits of the dead airmen completing the journey they never managed to finish in life?

RAF Coleby Grange

A story from RAF Coleby Grange rounds off this trip round Bomber County. Every May, the ghost of a guilt ridden RAF officer is supposed to return to haunt the site of the former RAF base at Coleby Grange, south of Lincoln. The legend says that in life the officer tormented himself over the number of young men he had sent on air raids, who had consequently been killed – one of whom had been his best friend. This mournful figure has been observed looking sadly from the top floor of the old control tower, his gaze taking in the overgrown runway. Mysterious footsteps have also been heard in the top corridor. Sometime in the mid-1990s, two friends visited Coleby Grange and found the control tower 'colder than the grave'. As they wandered around they felt as if they were being watched, and as they went upstairs the hairs on the backs of their necks stood up – for it sounded as if footsteps were following them up the metal stairs. Looking back, they saw no one to account for the noises. One of the boys left a coin on the stairs as they ascended; as they returned downstairs it was gone. However, they did find the coin again – unaccountably left for them in the doorway, to be found as they exited the place.

However, Coleby has other alleged phantoms. The drone of long-gone bombers has been heard, and some kind of malignant spirit is held to throw stones at people outside looking up at the control tower. This is surely not the work of the tormented RAF officer.

Strangest of all, perhaps, are the curious headaches reported to be felt near the stairs. During a red alert a man is held to have fallen down the stairs and cracked his head, leading to his death. People have reported unaccountable head pains near this area and have been assailed by ghostly voices, thumps, bangs and other unusual noises.

In 2005, an all-night vigil by a six-member group of paranormal investigators named 'The Believe Team' was held at Coleby's control tower. One member described the atmosphere thus: 'This has to be one of the scariest places I've ever been to with The Believe Team. You know it's derelict, it doesn't feel comfortable, so I've got a feeling that this is going to be one scary evening.' It was. Thumps and bangs spooked the investigators, strange lights were spotted, and at 10.45 p.m. an unseen hand appeared to lob a rock at one member of the team. Digital cameras took photographs of strange misty white shapes – the fascinating 'orbs' that seem to crop up in photographs at allegedly haunted sites.

Phantom legions

It is thought to be the echoes of a battle fought in Saxon times that people claim to have heard at Battle Green in Epworth. Folklore says that the clashing of weapons and screams of pain can be heard, but perhaps the best evidence for the 'proof' of this phantom battle came from a woman who took early morning walks on Battle Green. This woman had attended the local ghost walk and had mentioned that on one occasion – very early in the misty morning – she had heard tremendous shouting and noises as though there was a football match playing on Battle Green. Some claim that it is the site of the defeat and beheading of King Oswald of Northumbria in AD 642, but he is thought to have been slain in battle with King Penda of Mercia somewhere in the Welsh Marches.

It is said that the impressive sight of Cromwell's Roundhead army has been seen marching along the Main Road in Saltfleet. Phantom echoes, perhaps, of when the man himself came to Saltfleet so his soldiers could root out Cavaliers in the surrounding marshes. But in Bourne the ghostly army is much, much older: for they say that a legion of Roman soldiers has been seen to make its way along Mill Drove.

Around 2004, a viewer contacted the BBC Lincolnshire homepage to relate how, as a teenager at his parent's home in the vicinity of Ermine Street, Lincoln, he awoke to the sound of footsoldiers marching. The night was very still, and the noises very clear; when he opened the window, the noises increased. After a minute or so the invisible army had passed and a shout was heard in the distance before all was quiet again.

Whilst one assumes that the spectral parade was that of a Roman legion, in Brigg the ghostly soldiers who are said to march along Wrawby Street are of a different calibre. For a band of men are said to still walk the street, retracing their journey that took them to war in 1914.

CHAPTER SIX

ANIMAL ENIGMAS

The Hare of Bolingbroke Castle

According to the seventeenth-century source the *Harleian MS*, Bolingbroke Castle was plagued by the appearance of a ghostly hare – if indeed a ghost it was. The castle, in the village of Old Bolingbroke, fell into disrepair after the English Civil War, but prior to that it was a proud example of thirteenth-century castle design famous for being the birthplace of Henry Bolingbroke, later King Henry IV of England.

The ancient text gives no clue as to the exact date of the haunting, but reading between the lines it appears the story was contemporary when the *Harleian MS* was written. Locals in the surrounding area believed the hare to be the spirit of a witch that had once been jailed in the castle.

It was recorded that the hare would put in unwanted appearances during meetings of auditors at the castle, where it would upset proceedings by running between their legs and sometimes overthrowing them. Those assembled would chase the strange animal into the castle yard and observe it dart through a grate and into a low cellar – whereupon they would enter themselves with torches to capture the trapped hare. However, the animal would vanish – despite the cellar being of solid stone and there being no exit from which the hare could escape. Dogs that chased the hare were found whimpering with terror after the hare had vanished in front of them during the chase.

These days, Bolingbroke Castle is a dilapidated ruin, and all that remains are the ground floors of its towers and the lower layers of its walls. However, Heritage Lincolnshire – who manages the site – may be interested to know that despite the passing centuries the hare has still, allegedly, been glimpsed recently. Apparently, this takes place – appropriately enough – in March, although how the animal can be distinguished from a normal hare is anybody's guess!

The remains of a cellar at Bolingbroke Castle, ancient scene of the weirdest of hauntings.

Black Shuck, Hairy Jack and their Breed

On 4 August 1577, parishioners in Bungay, Suffolk, found themselves stuck in the village church – St Mary's – as a violent thunderstorm gathered overhead during the Sunday morning service.

The sky became black, and as the villagers sheltered from the appalling weather conditions something out of a nightmare invaded the church. Witnesses described how a fiery black dog crashed into the place and tore through the congregation. This monster bit two people by the throat and killed them; a third person was bitten on the back so that he 'shrivelled up like a piece of leather'. After the entity had finished its rampage the terrified parishioners emerged to find the church door ripped with what appeared to be claw marks, and the wheels and wires of the church clock were similarly found to be smashed and twisted. It appeared that this creature had attacked the church before it had finally succeeded in getting in to launch itself at those inside.

Seven miles away, at Blythburgh, this creature continued its rampage, attacking the local church there and wounding some of those inside. As in Bungay, it left claw marks and scratches on the church door.

That night in Suffolk is a particularly well-documented phenomenon. Locals blamed the attack on a hound from Hell – the demon dog known as Black Shuck. He has been reported from all parts of the British Isles; on the Isle of Man he is known as Moddey Dhoo, in Lancashire he is Trash or Skriker, in Staffordshire he is Padfoot, and in Scotland he is the Muckle Black. In Lincolnshire he is known as Hairy Jack.

Folklorists have claimed that black dogs in Lincolnshire are – by comparison to the aforementioned monster – harmless and even protective, but this is contentious. There is a wonderful tale of Black Shuck appearing out of nowhere to protect a woman being harassed by a gang of labourers as she walked home along the Scunthorpe to Crosby road in the twentieth century. The Shuck accompanied the woman to her home, whereupon it disappeared as suddenly as it had appeared. However, there is still a clear dividing line between the 'ghost dogs', such as Guy Gibson's pet, and the Black Shucks that roam the countryside and startle travellers. Although some of these beasts do not appear to present any particular threat, these apparitions are sometimes considered to be omens of doom (if you should spot the giant white dog of Digby you risk bad luck if you speak before you have seen a white horse!) and on occasion have been downright terrifying.

Such a creature – or creatures – haunts the fields and village lanes in an area that covers, roughly speaking, east of Gainsborough to the south of Scunthorpe. There is an undated story that tells how a farmer ploughing a field in Hemswell turned over the bones of a strange animal one day. Closer inspection revealed that the skull of the beast was the size of a donkey … yet its shape and teeth indicated that it had belonged to a dog. The farmer recovered the complete skeleton of the creature and brushed off the muck and dirt before putting it all into a sack: he then set off for home as darkness fell, intending to show his curious find to his friends at the village pub that evening.

Mist enshrouded the lane as the farmer walked home, and in the gloom behind him he became aware of the padding of footsteps following him. Turning, he saw to his terror that he was being stalked by a monstrous, enormous black dog that now began to run at him with its jaws salivating and its fangs bared in a ferocious canine snarl!

The farmer ran for his life but the creature easily caught up with him. As the dog bore down on his back, the farmer swung the sack at his pursuer; the sack burst open against the dog's head, and the skull was thrown into the lane where it shattered to pieces. With that the monster vanished in mid-leap and the farmer found himself alone in the empty lane.

Today, the lanes that connect Hemswell and Grayingham, some three miles to the north, are said to be haunted by immense black dogs the size of calves. Hairy Jack has been spotted at Willoughton, where in 1933 a giant dog with 'bristly skin' like a pig leapt up at a man and threw him back against a gatepost, and at Blyborough where a woman had a chilling encounter on the road by the village pond in Victorian times. Whilst out walking, she gradually became aware that she was being followed. Turning, she saw a black dog of great size stalking her and in blind fear she lashed out at it with an umbrella … which passed straight through the beast. The animal continued to stalk her before eventually growing bored and disappearing off into a field. There are notable similarities between this encounter and the one at Hemswell. Ethel Rudkin's book, *Folklore* (1938), claimed that apart from haunting the village pond Hairy Jack also lurked near the 'Old Yard' in the village. In the 1800s one Samuel Prettywell is alleged to have been so terrified by his encounter with a black dog that he tried to fire his gun at it. The weapon misfired and exploded, and although there was no doubt whisperings of supernatural intervention in the incident, perhaps this was just one dog of earthly origins that was very lucky not to have been shot that day.

The monstrous black dog of Hemswell; strange black dogs have prowled the Lincolnshire landscape for centuries.

The countryside of Dragonby, haunt of Hairy Jack. This odd rock formation within the hill is alleged to be a petrified dragon.

There are certain places the nation over where Black Shucks appear to prowl: lonely country lanes, crossroads, gateways, sites of buried treasure, and in some cases forests and hedges. More spiritually, they are also linked to ley lines, or leys, which take the form of arrow-straight alignments of ancient sites often stretching for miles across the landscape and passing through such sites as long barrows, churches, pagan burial grounds and prehistoric mounds. Here, the animal appears to be 'on patrol' as if protecting a boundary line for some unknown reason; at Bourne Wood, Bourne, a Black Shuck would sit on the edge of the tree-line watching travellers pass by through the forest. The beast was immense, but never broke out into the open, as though it was duty-bound to guard something and could not leave the protection of the tree line.

The lane that led up to Moortown House in Moortown, was patrolled by a big black dog that would always vanish into the hedge at the exact same spot. This beast frightened other animals: on one occasion a pony faltered in the lane after sensing the presence of the shuck. The hapless rider was forced to walk the rest of the way on his own.

Dragonby, a small village near Scunthorpe, is associated with the phenomenon of ley lines – perhaps this is why spectral black dogs are reputed to haunt Dragonby hill fort.

Similarly, a trackway at Kirton-in-Lindsey where Hairy Jack is said to prowl is reputedly on a ley line. In the 1930s a schoolmistress reported that she had seen the eerie beast loping along the verge of a lane between Kirton-in-Lindsey and Manton. One wonders if this is the same black canine that is said to have caused mayhem at a police station in Lindsey by prowling about the place – allegedly passing through walls.

Another popular haunt of black dogs seems to be near water: streams, bridges and ponds. A Black Shuck pads around the Wrawby Road bridge at Brigg, North Lincolnshire, and legend has it that he appears on a Saturday night for some unknown reason. A similar entity has been spotted lying in wait at a bridge between Manton and Scotter; and such a creature also patrols the bridge over the River Till at Willingham. An account of the sinister side of Hairy Jack comes from Kirton-in-Lindsey in the 1930s: a giant black hound made its home in a hole in the banks of the River Eau, near to Belle Hole Farm. On one occasion this monster entered the farmhouse kitchen – the farmer's wife, paralysed with fear, dared not move until the beast loped off on its own free will. Despite the farmer's efforts to block the hole where the dog 'lived' it continued to plague them, often frightening the children. When the couple's children told their nursemaid of the spectral creature she laughed it off as a fairytale, until the animal presented itself to her within Belle Hole Farm after somehow getting in. It is an indictment of the folktale element of the black dog legend that this incident is also reputed to have occurred in the 1800s as well as the 1930s.

Ethel Rudkin collected many tales of ghostly black dogs for her 1938 publication *Folklore*. She talked to many people in her native Lincolnshire about the topic and commented, 'Perhaps it is because I have seen the black dog, and can therefore believe that the narrator has also seen him, that I have been able to get such good first-hand stories.' She also commented that none of the witnesses she talked to appeared to be weak minded – but unfortunately she does not elaborate on her own run-in with Hairy Jack.

Rudkin formed the impression that black dogs in Lincolnshire were in the main of a gentle nature compared to some others reported around the UK. It was looked upon as a kind of spiritual protector, a large hound that would often appear to the left of a witness, crossing the road from left to right. Confusingly for an animal that was apparently ethereal, it made the bushes rustle when it vanished into a hedgerow. And, Rudkin pointed out, no matter how dark the night Hairy Jack would always be seen – because he was so much blacker than the darkness.

Although Ethel Rudkin established that the black dogs of Lincolnshire were generally benevolent, it appears that the spectral hounds *can* be downright menacing, as indicated in some of the tales above. Thus in Lincolnshire at least, it can be said that Black Shuck takes many roles. From the true 'Hound of Hell' to the sinister, lurking black dog, to the protective benefactor, whatever form he takes he is a collective piece of Lincolnshire folklore, and by 1958 folklorists had ascertained that there were some forty-seven haunts of black dogs in the county of Lincolnshire.

Hairy Jack is still very much with us. In Spalding in 1974, a young boy of five years of age endured a terrifying night-time sighting of Black Shuck. After a couple of hours asleep, the child was awoken by the sound of feet padding outside his bedroom. Thinking it was the family dog, the boy raised his head above the sheets – and was confronted by a truly frightening vision of a demon dog in the corridor outside. The monster was some 3ft tall, and its coat stood on end. Its teeth were bared in a vicious canine snarl as it bounded along the landing towards the boy's bedroom door. The dog was truly massive, with a black coat and the oft-repeated blazing saucer-like yellow eyes. The snarling beast vanished in front of the cowering boy as it reached his bedroom threshold. Although the age of the witness gives doubt to the credibility of this story, it should be pointed out that the boy is now a doctor, Dr Simon Sherwood, who has lectured at both Edinburgh and Northampton Universities, and his experience has generated a lifelong interest in the pursuit of the black dog mystery. This story is significant; for it indicates that the beast is still around in Lincolnshire and can invade homes if it wishes.

In 1982 Richard Jones had an unsettling encounter with a black dog. Richard was driving through Faldingworth accompanied by a friend, when they saw the dark shape of a dog emerge from the hedgerows up ahead. The beast slowly padded out into the middle of the road, stopped and turned its head to look at the approaching vehicle. From a distance of 50ft, Richard and his friend were startled to see that the animal had no eyes or features; indeed, it appeared to have no face at all; he described it as being 'like a deep black vivid shadow'. As they drew nearer, the black dog simply vanished in front of them.

In North Lincolnshire, a Shuck was allegedly seen in 1983 near Barton-upon-Humber. But perhaps the most recent sighting of Hairy Jack comes from the suitably imposing setting of Thornton Abbey, near East Halton in North Lincolnshire. Founded in the eleventh century by Augustinian monks, the massive castellated gatehouse and moat were added in the fourteenth century and enclose what little remains of the abbey itself. Sunken eyed gargoyles and statues eye the visitor who passes through the enormous gatehouse.

Such visitors included Jenny Jones and her mother, who visited the abbey one afternoon in 2000. Looking up at one of the gatehouse windows, Jenny saw what she thought may have been a ghost: a middle-aged woman with brown tied back hair, whom Jenny 'sensed' wished them to leave. At that point a great black Labrador appeared from nowhere and ran at Jenny and her mother, who both turned and fled in the direction of the car. Jenny claims that they ran through the gatehouse and suddenly found the aggressive beast *in front* of them somehow. It chased them to the car, and then watched them as they drove away. Jenny claims that once it was satisfied they had gone away it trotted back towards the gatehouse … and 'disappeared completely'.

But does this demon dog of the wild countryside have a master? One of the oldest reports of the dogs from Hell seems to suggest so.

The first English black dog account is generally considered to be the one given in the *Anglo-Saxon Chronicle* in the year 1127. Abbot Henry of Poitou had recently arrived with his retinue at Peterborough Abbey, and on the following Sunday after his arrival, during hymns, many men saw and heard a great number of huntsmen. They were first glimpsed charging through the deer park in Peterborough and then through the forest known as Burghley Woods, that stretched all the

The imposing entrance to Thornton Abbey, near East Halton.

way to Stamford. The huntsmen terrified the locals; they were demonic, huge and hideous. They rode black horses and black male goats as they crashed through the woodland, and this ghastly hunt was accompanied by terrifying, jet-black hounds whose eyes blazed like saucers. Vigilant watchers claimed that there were some thirty huntsmen, and the monks at Peterborough Abbey heard the diabolical huntsmen sounding and winding their horns every night from the date of the abbot's arrival, through Lent and up until Easter. This experience was written as fact at the time, not only in the *Anglo Saxon Chronicle* but also by Hugh Candidus of Peterborough. The demonic hunt was seen and heard by many persons of unquestioned veracity and apparently the story spread nationwide.

Although there are clear religious overtones to this tale, could it be that this is how Hairy Jack, Black Shuck and their breed started life? As demon dogs that accompanied mysterious, unknown huntsmen that petrified the inhabitants of Peterborough and south Lincolnshire … before the entire ghastly hunt thundered off, back to wherever it was they had come from?

The Dam Busters mascot that still wags its tail

The big black Labrador that trotted around after his master at RAF Scampton was already a legend in his own lifetime for the flyers stationed there during the Second World War, long

Guy Gibson teases his faithful companion with a pipe. This image can be found in the RAF Scampton Historical Museum.

before he had passed into Dam Buster folklore: for he was Nigger, and despite his unfortunate name, he was the inseparable companion of the legendary leader of that famous raid, Wing Commander Guy Gibson. The friendly animal had been with the flying ace when he had served at Digby and Coningsby, and had accompanied him when he came to RAF Scampton to form the Dam Busters squadron that would go on to launch the devastating 'bouncing bomb' raids on the six dams in Germany's industrial heartland of the Ruhr.

Tradition says Nigger was loved by all at RAF Scampton: he became the base's mascot, and his name was chosen as the code word that the flyers would radio in to announce they had destroyed the Mohne dam; in the run up to the endeavour the faithful hound would be treated to halves of bitter and the occasional puff on Gibson's pipe in the mess.

The raid on the dam was scheduled for the night of 16 May 1943. On the evening before, just as Gibson had finished a final debriefing session with his flight commanders and bomb aimers, he was approached and sombrely informed that Nigger was dead; the unfortunate animal had been killed by a car outside the main gate to RAF Scampton.

The accident left Gibson seriously depressed at the death of his old companion, and he understandably tried to keep Nigger's death secret from the crew and personnel at Scampton. It could hardly bode well if the team's mascot had been killed on the evening before the crucial and dangerous attack on Germany.

Nigger's grave stands before Gibson's old quarters and looks out upon RAF Scampton's runway.

Nevertheless, the following night nineteen Lancasters took off from the grassy runways of Scampton on their mission, and in waves pounded four of their six targets in the Ruhr with giant drum-shaped 'bouncing bombs'. The bombs tore huge holes in the Mohne and Eder dams and released millions of gallons of vital water that the industrial Ruhr depended on. The raid was a spectacular success – but it came at a price. Eight Lancasters were lost, and 53 of the 133 crew died during the mission.

At around the time the team were attacking Germany, back at Scampton Gibson's faithful pet was buried in the grassy ground surrounding one of the hangars. It was midnight, and the hound was buried in accordance with Gibson's instructions.

Long after the carnage of war had finished, strange incidents concerning a black Labrador dog were reported around the area.

In February 1952, a mess waiter was sitting alone in a downstairs staffroom one afternoon when his eyes fell upon a medium-sized black Labrador sitting in the yard outside. The animal was looking up at the upper windows of the officer's mess building, at Gibson's old quarters, and was completely motionless. The airman, his curiosity aroused, left the staffroom and ventured outside – an act that took a matter of seconds – only to find that the Labrador had vanished, with no explanation of how it could have taken off so fast: in all directions, had it run off, it should still have been visible, if only as a fleeing shape…

Two days later, the same airman was ordered by a Corporal to go and evict an unwanted intruder from the dining hall corridor – a black Labrador had somehow made its way inside the building. This time the dog took off when approached, and raced up some stairs to the first floor. The airman bounded up the stairs, but to his utter amazement the curious canine had performed another vanishing trick. Somehow it had got away, though all the doors were closed and it's only escape route was back down the stairs and past its pursuer!

In the following months the dog put in more unexplainable appearances. It was spotted bounding across a field and past the officer's mess by startled staff; when they went outside they noticed that although there had been a light fall of snow the dog had left no paw prints. After this the dog continued to be spotted, but never again in the clarity of daylight – from then on all sightings of it were made in the gathering gloom of night.

Later that year, USAF personnel stationed at RAF Scampton reported seeing the mysterious black Labrador, and by now airmen at the base were beginning to speculate that it was the ghost of Guy Gibson's dog, Nigger. Ten years to the day after the Dam Busters raid – the night of 16/17 May 1953 – an NCO and his wife saw a black Labrador dog run soundlessly past the main gate at dusk and out onto the road. When they walked out through the camp gates themselves, the dog was nowhere to be seen.

The following year, word spread quickly amongst the crew filming the classic British war film *The Dam Busters* at RAF Scampton that the dog that 'played' Nigger would shy away from passing Nigger's grave, afraid and cowed.

Sightings of the strange black Labrador persisted over the decades, around the airbase or more poignantly on the A15 road outside. In May 1983, a visitor to RAF Scampton reported that as he drove around the grounds and pulled up alongside Nigger's grave his pet dachshund, which was in the vehicle, became extremely upset and agitated. The frightened pet began throwing itself around the car and at the windows in an effort to break free, and only calmed down when the witness drove on.

Nigger's place in Lincolnshire's wartime history was already established while he was still alive, but his place in its paranormal folklore is now indisputable thanks to a bizarre event that took place in the centre of Woodhall Spa in 1987. Woodhall Spa was the Dam Busters' subsequent base after RAF Scampton, and 17 May of that year was the day chosen to unveil a memorial to the heroic Dam Busters of 617 Squadron. The choir of St Hugh's school led the singing in front of the memorial on the special occasion.

Due to the bad weather, the service was finished without any official photographs of the scarlet-cassocked children being taken as souvenirs. So, a few days afterwards, when the weather was bright and sunny, the headmaster of St Hugh's took the children back to the memorial to have their photographs taken to remember the event. The children lined up in two rows in front of the memorial, with the front row seated and the back row standing. As they did so, a black Labrador proudly trotted in amongst those assembled and insisted on sitting with the children for the photograph.

Various attempts were made to shoo the dog on, and bribe him away from the children; but each time things settled down the dog quietly retook his position amongst the youngsters, patiently waiting for the photographer to get on with his job. Finally the photographer gave up and took a fine colour photograph of the children in their finery … with the black Labrador sat right at the front in the middle, looking directly at the camera.

A story like this may be said to be too good to be true, and a local journalist claimed that he had afterwards tracked the mystery pooch to a nearby house and owner; however a subsequent legend has turned up claiming a similar incident took place in the 1940s when a photographer tried to take a picture of assembled airmen at RAF Scampton – and a mysterious black Labrador had somehow gotten himself included in the photograph.

But it matters little to the mythology of Nigger. If the animal at Woodhall Spa was not Nigger, then it was surely one of the most extraordinary coincidences in the history of the Dam Busters saga and merely adds to the legend of Guy Gibson's companion. These days, RAF Scampton is home to the world-famous Red Arrows aerobatic display team. Nigger's grave is still on the site, where a plaque has been erected in honour of the Labrador. Railings have also been erected around the plot to deter souvenir hunters. There has been some suggestion of moving Nigger's remains to Steenbergen in the Netherlands … where his master, Guy Gibson is buried.

The Phantom Herd

Twenty-two-year-old Bob Harvet was driving home one night in 1972. He was following the roads around Grantham, including one allegedly haunted road called The Four Wheel, named after a stagecoach. As he drove, the road became enshrouded with fog, but when he pulled over and got out Bob discovered that the fog only came up to his chest. In the darkness Bob found himself slightly disorientated; the countryside around him was blanked by the bizarre chest-high fog, while the clear starry sky was clearly visible above his head.

As he stood in the silence he heard a distant howl, a noise that prompted a cluster of birds to take off in flight. Bob stood uneasily for a few minutes and then slowly became aware of the steady sound of approaching hoof beats – thundering along The Four Wheels and heading towards his car!

The noise charged past the young man and then continued along the road up ahead of him, growing ever distant. The fog remained unbroken.

Shivering, Bob got back into his car to turn on the heater. As he sat there, the nearby sound of animal noises – grunting and snuffling – made the hairs on the back of his neck stand up. He turned the engine off to listen more closely, at which point the car began to rock and jostle as though a herd of invisible animals was moving past it in the fog. Bob's car was open-topped, and in the gloom of the night he saw nothing to account for any of the sounds or buffeting.

As suddenly as it had begun, the activity ceased and the lane was peaceful again. Shaken, Bob turned his car around and headed back to Grantham where he booked himself into a hotel. In subsequent years he drove along the road many, many times … but never again was his bizarre experience repeated.

Invisible to Man

From Bottesford, a little place on the southern outskirts of Scunthorpe, comes a local tale of a ghost that haunts a spot along Bottesford Beck. This legend is markedly different to others in that animals alone appear to see the spook.

At some point the beck had been the scene of an outrage, when a servant girl making her way to a farm was attacked and murdered. For some time afterwards horses were reputed to become nervous as they cantered along the road; at the point where a crossing took them over the beck they would stall in the road and quite often turn around, along with the wagons or traps they were pulling. Handlers and owners would frequently have to dismount in order to cajole the frightened animals over the crossing.

But it wasn't only the horses. Cattle in the adjacent field would give the crossing point a wide berth, and it was thought that they also saw something that the humans didn't – could it be the shade of the murdered girl?

Interestingly, there is a field in Osgodby, near Market Rasen, that similarly frightens horses. Riders who have taken their mount along Washdyke Lane, off Main Street, to the bend have reported that strange things happen once they have left the lane and gone into the field. The horses appear to become irrational, frightened by something that they can sense in the field. Often they will abruptly cease their cantering and refuse to go any further, despite being spurred on.

Some people have also reported that this particular field, to the left of the bend in the lane, has an extremely oppressive, heavy atmosphere, as though something is not at all right.

Trickster spirits

Possibly the weirdest of the entities that are said to roam the Lincolnshire countryside is the bizarre apparition known as the Shag Foal. This creature's stomping ground is Kirton-in-Lindsey, to the south of Scunthorpe, North Lincolnshire.

The Shag Foal takes the form of a donkey with fiery, blazing eyes; some describe it as merely a 'phantom' creature - but there may be more to this oddity. In her book *County Folklore* (1908), folklorist Miss M.G.W. Peacock described the Shag Foal – sometimes referred to as the Tatter Foal or Tatter Colt – as a shape-shifting goblin who chose to take the form of a small horse or a donkey with a rough, scruffy coat. This creature used to haunt the fens and wetlands before the technology of drainage took away its playground; it would appear to travellers in this inhospitable environment and lure or trick them into streams and swamps. When the tourist had become lost or up to his neck in water the Shag Foal would drift away with a prolonged outburst of laughter which was half horse's whinny and half human mockery.

North of Scunthorpe, around the area of Barton-upon-Humber, this creature was referred to as the Tatter Foal: a rough coated horse with glowing red eyes that lurked in the surrounding marshes. Like its counterpart further south it lured travellers and children to a watery death in the marshlands. Rather than a horse's whinny or neighing, the Tatter Foal made a terrifying noise that sounded like grating coffin lid or iron chains rattling.

Sightings of this creature gradually died away, and what it was – a will o' the-wisp, a goblin in disguise or some sort of curious ghost animal – is somewhat unclear. However, towards the end of the nineteenth century there were reports that a spectral white calf haunted the road between Wrawby and Brigg. The thing had appeared to travellers and earned the name 'the lackey causey calf' (in other words the leaky causeway calf) because it appeared to be luring those unlucky enough to come across away from the main roads. This entity would seem to be a local variant on the Shag Foal creature – albeit a little more modern in the telling.

CHAPTER SEVEN

A HAUNTED COUNTY

Nine Tongues Within One Head – The Story of Tom Otter's Ghost

Tom Otter was a man in trouble. He was already a family man, with a wife and child in Southwell, Nottinghamshire; yet, whilst working as a navvy on the enclosure of the Swanpool in Lincoln, he had become romantically entangled with a girl named Mary Kirkham from North Hykeham.

Mary Kirkham had fallen pregnant and a shotgun wedding was arranged. The reason behind this was that, in 1805, a child born with no legal father would become the financial responsibility of the local parish – thus the marriage was forced by the authorities. With the authorities unaware he was already married, Otter had to decide whether to go through with the wedding or face going to prison. So, on 3 November 1805, parish constables escorted the twenty-eight-year-old navvy on his happy occasion to South Hykeham, where the ceremony was performed.

After leaving the church, Otter and his new bride were seen walking along the old turnpike through Saxilby, in the direction of Drinsey Nook. At around 7.00 p.m. the couple sat down to rest at the roadside of what is now the B1190 Doddington Road, and in the darkness Otter grabbed a stake he had torn from a hedge and bashed poor Mary's brains out. He then tipped her body into a ditch that ran alongside the road.

Mary's corpse was found the following morning and taken back to Saxilby, where it was laid out at the Sun Inn. Otter was himself arrested in Lincoln and returned to Saxilby for the inquest. Here, a constable noticed that sunlight from a window that shone upon Otter illuminated what appeared to be bloodstains he had tried to wash out of his clothes.

The trial at Lincoln Castle learned that Otter's real name was Temporell, or possibly Temple, and also of his second family in Nottinghamshire. The motive for the crime was clear and he was sentenced to death on 12 March 1806, the whole process apparently being facilitated by a confession he was alleged to have made. The following week he was strung up and hanged in

A view of Gibbet Wood, off Tom Otter's Lane (the B1190 Doddington road)

Lincoln in front of a huge crowd. After the execution, many more villagers and locals swarmed to Drinsey Nook to watch the gibbeting of the corpse on 20 March.

Tom's body was brought from Lincoln, and his corpse suspended in a steel cage 30ft off the ground at a spot 100 yards from the place where he had murdered Mary Kirkham. His corpse was left to rot away and serve as a reminder to all who passed by of the power of the law. It was also a gruesome testament to the memory of the unfortunate victim.

At the time, gibbets swung gently in the wind at many a turnpike or footway across the country. Tom Otter's body remained suspended at the site for years; he was the last person in Lincolnshire to be gibbeted, and the story should have ended there. But it did not. Tom Otter's name entered into the annals of Lincolnshire folklore; after all, it is not often that a wife is slain by her husband on their wedding day. But there were other, more superstitious reasons too.

After Mary Kirkham's body had been found, it was taken in a cart to the Sun Inn, Saxilby. It was said that there had been no straw laid out in the cart to soak up the blood and as a result the wheels left a gruesome trail of gore in its tracks as the body was taken over the drawbridge at the Fossdyke canal and up the steps of the inn. According to legend, servant girls tried in vain for years to clean the blood-soaked doorsteps, yet no amount of scrubbing would remove them, and many quit their jobs because of it. Furthermore, on the anniversary of the murder, the room where Mary's body had been laid out echoed with the pathetic, ghostly crying of a newborn infant.

When Otter's corpse was gibbeted on 20 March, the event seemed jinxed. After the cart carrying the iron-clad body clattered over Saxilby drawbridge, the drawbridge broke down; and in the surge to see the gibbet hoisted aloft several people were crushed and injured. The gibbet was erected in high winds, and twice the tackle with which the men attempted to raise it broke. One man, struck by the collapsing beam, stated that now the gibbet was aloft Tom Otter would stay put up there. But the contraption collapsed a third time in the gales and the iron-clad body of the killer fell onto the same unfortunate man. As he was being taken away from the scene, the man wailed how he was a doomed man because Tom Otter had cursed him for appearing as a prosecution witness: that same man died of his injuries the very next day.

The Foss Dyke, passing by the Sun Hotel in Saxilby, c. 1900.

The bloodstained hedge stake that had been used as a murder weapon had been displayed as a gruesome curiosity at the Sun Inn. Yet on the first anniversary of the killing it vanished from the inn, and was found in the same field at the same spot where Otter had tossed it after carrying out the murder. This happened two years running, so the stake was removed from the inn to another at Torksey Lock where it was fastened to the wall by iron hoops. Yet, on 3 November, it once again vanished in the night, torn away again by some supernatural force.

The hedge stake next passed to the Peewit Inn, further along the Fossdyke, where the landlord secured it to the wall with three strong staples. Yet on the night of the anniversary of the murder it again vanished … and, even more frightening, on this occasion the staples came crashing through the landlord's bedroom window, thrown by someone – or something – unknown. The landlord, one Richard Naylor, had helped to make the iron gibbet in which Otter's body now swung at Drinsey Nook. And so it went on, until one night, on the anniversary of the murder, a party of locals determined to find out what was happening, had the idea of sitting all night round the stake (once again attached securely to the wall of the Peewit Inn). But during the night a strange deep sleep overtook them – and when they awoke, the stake had been torn away once again and tossed in the field.

It was whispered that every time the stake was retrieved it would be wet with fresh blood, and at this the Bishop of Lincoln decided to end the matter. He declared the relic a symbol of evil and superstition and had it burned secretly one night in the Minster yard.

Over the years, the lane where the gibbet swung became known as Tom Otter's Lane, and the nearby woodland was nicknamed Gibbet Wood. As the corpse rotted away the jawbone fell open, revealing inside the gaping mouth a bird's nest containing a cluster of chicks. Even by the end of the nineteenth century a local rhyme celebrating this bizarre wildlife habitat could be recited by some: 'There were nine tongues within one head; The tenth went out to seek for bread; To feed the living within the dead'. Souvenir hunters and the elements chipped away at the gibbet until, in 1850, it collapsed totally. It is said that the iron from the gibbet was used to make, of all things, a chair for a local doctor.

Still the tale of Tom Otter refused to die. Years later, a dying man named John Dunberly (or Dunkerly, or Dunkley) allegedly made a bizarre deathbed confession at his home in Doddington in the presence of a parson. Unless a total fabrication, it provided the answer to the mystery of who had kept throwing the stake into the field on each anniversary of the murder…

Dunberly claimed that on the evening of the murder back in November 1805 he had made his way out of the Ship Inn at around six in the evening, some ten minutes after Otter and his new wife had passed by. On his way back to Doddington he had passed some acquaintances who shouted at him that he would have company on his way home, for Otter and the girl had just passed down Drinsey Nook lane in the direction of Doddington. Dunberly, in his confession, admitted he was something of a Peeping Tom who got his kicks from spying on courting couples: so he trailed the newlyweds until he espied them up ahead about to take a rest. Dunberly threw himself through the hedgerow and snuck up on the couple until nothing but a hedge divided them.

But there was to be no mischief between the couple. Dunberly watched in horror as Otter wrenched a stake out of the hedge and muttered to himself, 'This will finish my knob-stick wedding'. He then saw Otter proceed to bash Mary's head in as she sat slumped in tiredness.

Dunberly had fainted. Upon coming round he found the hedge stake lying near him in the field where Otter had thrown it, and gingerly he picked it up. When he found his hands were covered in blood he fled the scene and for some time left the area – afraid of being implicated in the killing. When he returned the murder trial was over, and Otter had been executed.

Dunberley made his way to Drinsey Nook to see the iron gibbet being hoisted up the beam, and when the ghastly contraption fell in the wind the first time he made to help the men lift it back up. At this moment the hairs on his head stood up, for as the cage was being wrestled back up Dunberly placed his hand on the corpse inside … and the cold, dead hand of Otter grabbed his so tightly that it left finger marks for weeks afterwards.

In the months following Mary's murder, Dunberley often found himself tottering home after a night at the Sun Inn and as usual he would glance up at the rotting corpse swinging in the wind 30ft above him. On some occasions he thought he had seen Otter shake his head at him as he passed by underneath; on a different occasion he had commented to the body, 'You gave me a bit of a turn once with your eyes and made my hand quite bad, but you'll not do nowt at me no more'. At this the corpse kicked it's leg and, according to Dunberly, would have sent one of his shank bones flying towards the drunk's head had it not been fastened to the iron. After that, he had always walked on the other side of the road.

On the first anniversary of the murder, Dunberly found himself unaccountably tired and fell into a deep, troubled sleep whilst on his own at home. At some point in the night he claimed to have been woken by the ghost of Tom Otter standing before him, who commanded, 'It's time. Come along.' As if in a dream, Dunberly had calmly followed the ghost to the Sun Inn, where Otter had ordered him to get the hedge stake from inside. Outside, the ghost of Mary Kirkham had joined Otter. Both were dressed in the same clothes they had worn on the night of the murder, and Mary carried a paper box in one hand and a pair of clogs in the other. All then proceeded in 'a kind of misty twilight' down Drinsey Nook lane.

At the spot where the murder had taken place, the grim scene was re-enacted, with Mary sitting down and hanging her head low in her tiredness. But Otter's ghost barked at Dunberly to get on with it quickly: and at this Dunberly felt compelled to beat the woman to death, taking Otter's role as murderer in the dark silence of the country lane.

Every year, on the anniversary of the murder, the same course of actions were played out. Otter would come for Dunberly, and they would always steal the stake (at the Peewit Inn, Otter had helped him prise the staples off the wall). Then he would re-enact the killing, taking Otter's role as murderer before throwing away the hedge stake and fainting into the hedgerow. He would always wake up with blood on his hands. His torment continued until the Bishop of Lincoln ordered the hedge stake destroyed, after which the ghosts never again came for Dunberly.

All of it sounds like the deathbed ramblings of a drunk who had become obsessed by the corpse he saw hanging in the country lane as he passed by every night, and the only ghosts who plagued him were perhaps in his mind. Perhaps Dunberly heard of the ghosts that were supposed to haunt the Sun Inn, and listened blearily to the tales of ghostly apparitions that landlords swore they had seen floating through the place. Others told how unaccountable knockings and bashings would wake those in the Sun Inn from their slumbers, or how things would vanish and then reappear mysteriously in a totally arbitrary place. Alternatively the whole tale could have been a fabrication invented by the clergyman who was at Dunberly's deathbed. But it is the nearest thing to an explanation – such as it is – for the bizarre disappearance of the bloodstained hedge stake.

Caistor's Clerical Conundrums

Legend has it that in the nineteenth century the vicar of Caistor, the Revd George Watson, earned a reputation for himself. He would ride out to parishioners in remote villages, and soon whispers began that he was having an affair with a widow whose stable he used. A subsequent inquiry exonerated Watson of any wrongdoing, but it was too late – Watson had killed himself, suffering from chronic depression. The unhappy vicar was buried in the south aisle of St Peter and St Paul's church.

Before long it was said that the ghost of the vicar walked the vicarage, with reports of the clergyman passing the two large French windows towards the house door. A family who lived at the vicarage all claimed to have seen the ghost of a vicar, dressed in grey, and hearing the sound of doors mysteriously opening when all was quiet.

This spectre is apparently distinct from the phantom monk who locals say plays the organ in the adjacent church. In January 1967, Canon Ernest Pitman attempted to lay the story to rest for good, claiming it to be a piece of superstitious folklore. He left a tape recorder overnight in the church and locked the door. When he recovered the tape recorder the next day and played the recording back, he was shocked by what he heard… footsteps that echoed through the empty building, banging noises and loud, clear notes that clearly came from the church organ…

The Ruskington Horror

The first the world heard of the so-called Ruskington Horror was in 1998. The popular daytime television show, *This Morning*, was chairing a debate on the existence of ghosts in the company of hosts Richard Madeley and Julia Carling, and guest expert the Revd Lionel Fanthorpe. One caller, Kevin Whelan from Lincolnshire, rang in to recount his tale of the supernatural; it was a terrifying account that opened the floodgates for others to come forward with their own reports.

Some two weeks previously, Mr Whelan recalled, he had been driving home from Lincoln to Sleaford along the A15. It was 2.00 a.m. on a Sunday in mid-January, and the A15 was quiet with the still of the night.

Just before the turn-off left to Ruskington, he spotted something like a 'white shadow' (in a later interview he described it as looking like a floating white bin bag) in the road ahead. When he reached it he suddenly became aware of a face forming at the driver's side window, and before he knew it something was glaring into the windscreen. For about forty to fifty seconds Mr Whelan stared into what he described as the face of a dark-haired Greek-looking person, who bared his teeth and whose olive skin was pitted green. Mr Whelan described it thus: 'From the neck down it was sort of … when you photograph someone with a flash on, it's too bright and you get that white fluorescent sort of look.' He also noticed that the creature's left hand was raised.

He continued driving at around sixty miles an hour, whilst in his fright attempting to shut off the tape player, which was playing music loudly, when the thing faded away down the side of the car. Mr Whelan told the show that he arrived home in a state of extreme distress, but once he had accepted the reality of his frightening encounter he had since returned to the spot with a video camera to try to find the thing again – without success.

During the rest of the show, two more callers phoned in and claimed that they too had been terrified by some kind of entity on the A15, just before the Ruskington road. A poultry deliveryman testified that in October or November 1984, whilst he was passing that same stretch of road, a dark figure with its hand raised walked out into the road. The witness floored his vehicle.

The third caller claimed that in 1996 a dark silhouette of a man ran out from a ditch in front of her car as she and her partner made their way back to Cranwell. The car bore down on the figure but hit nothing, and the witness's boyfriend – who was driving – appeared not to see the dark shape.

The following day Richard Madeley told *This Morning* viewers that Kevin Whelan's chilling account had prompted a flood of similar calls to the show's switchboard – some five dozen in all, with all the callers claiming to have had similar experiences at the same point in the road. All the reports followed broadly similar lines (the raised hand seemed to be a particularly repetitive detail), and one witness had even reported an incident as far back as 1960. He had been a school coach driver, and he had searched the road for a body after he apparently ran someone down – but no one was to be found.

An investigation by the *This Morning* team threw up possible candidates for the entity: a reputed motorcycle crash victim, a hermit run over and killed by an army lorry during the Second World War, and a highwayman who used to attack stagecoaches. Yet the A15 is a long stretch of road and has seen many accidents; one is left feeling that perhaps this story has not yet run its course.

For those who wish to see for themselves, the precise location of the encounters is past a house on the right as you head southbound, immediately before the left turn to Ruskington.

Kevin Whelan noted that the apparition had appeared, 'very, very, very distressed.' *This Morning* co-host, Julia Carling, speculated that if the apparition were that of a road accident victim then perhaps its behaviour was an attempt to prevent another tragedy on the A15. 'I don't know actually', commented Richard Madeley in reply, 'It frightens them.'

The Phantom Smoker

A man contacted BBC Lincolnshire's homepage with a bizarre tale of his brush with the supernatural. He had been drinking in the Monks Arms at Caenby Corner, and upon leaving had a lengthy walk back to his home in Blyborough. Although it was a good trek, it was a warm summer's evening.

On reaching Willoughton Top, where the road rises to Blyborough Top, he came across a man sitting against a tree smoking a cigarette. The man appeared oblivious to the approaching witness, and ignored his friendly, 'Good morning!'

Standing right in front of the man, he asked him if he was OK; still no response, the man simply continued smoking his cigarette. The witness was now becoming a little unnerved, so he bade the smoker cheerio and gave him 'a friendly tap' on his outstretched foot.

To his horror his shoe passed right through the man's leg, and at this the witness ran off in fear, not stopping until he got to Blyborough. As he reached his driveway, out of breath and as white as a sheet, he looked back up the hill from where he had run.

Terrified, he saw that the 'man' had followed him. But what floated down the hill after him was only a head and body – no legs or feet. Screaming, the witness ran into his house and slammed the door. He ended his report, 'I have never been so terrified in all my life.' And understandably so.

Stalked by the Old Hag

On the evening of 20 July 2000, three teenage boys claimed an inexplicable encounter with the ghost of an old woman in Boston. All three boys were due to stay overnight in the same house, and as they made their way along Mill Road towards the house one of them gave a start. Up in the branches of a nearby tree was a sinister-looking woman staring down at them.

Frightened, the group of lads avoided eye contact with the old woman and continued on past the tree. When they glanced back, she was no longer there.

The three boys, already a little unnerved, rounded a corner and to their shock saw the old woman in the path up ahead of them. As they nervously approached they were afforded quite a good view of her: the woman was quite old-looking and had short ginger hair. She wore a heavy, long black hooded coat and carried a large cross in front of her. Now thoroughly frightened, the boys passed her on the path before running all the way to the house where they were to spend the night.

The excitement of the strange incident was forgotten as the night drew on and the boys retired to sleep. But during the small hours one boy was awoken by a tap-tapping on the window pane, and he gingerly made his way to the window, heart pounding.

Drawing back the curtain, the lad found the strange old woman standing outside in the semi-darkness, tapping on the window, and still holding the large cross. Speechless with fright, it was all the lad could do to turn around and mouth silence at his two sleeping friends; when he turned back again, the old woman had vanished from the window.

None of the three boys ever saw this old woman again, or received an explanation for what it might have all been about.

Above left: An *image of the Boston Stump in days gone by.*

Above right: The Ross Tiger, *secured in Alexandra Dock by the National Fishing Heritage Centre.*

It is difficult to know what to make of this story, as it was posted on the internet by way of a friend-of-a-friend scenario. But the fifteen-year-old girl who submitted the story, 'Teena', claimed to have personally known the three boys to whom this experience happened. It is not inconceivable that the three boys, egging each other on during their sleepover, decided to 'invent' a scary story to regale their chums with, and Teena was sufficiently impressed by it to post it on the internet. On the other hand, just because all those concerned are adolescents, does not mean that something strange did not happen to them. After all, the tale is no stranger than Boston's 'traditional' ghost story: that of a phantom woman holding a baby who is reported to throw herself off the 272ft-high octagonal tower of St Botolph's church (known as the Boston Stump) in the Market Place on autumnal evenings.

Modern Haunts in Grimsby

For some reason the great fishing port of Grimsby seems to be producing the area's most unexpected modern locations for ghostly activity. The trend can be traced back to 16 November 2000, when the *Grimsby Evening Telegraph* ran a story that an Asda supermarket in Grimsby was home to a ghost. The ghost generally appeared in the evening, and, soon after an infrared security camera had been installed, its motion sensor was triggered by movement within the office one night. The camera started rolling and recorded what appeared to be the outline of a figure moving backwards and forwards within the office.

On 13 January 2005 the *Grimsby Evening Telegraph* reported another modern building that was allegedly haunted – the Index store in Freshney Place, Grimsby. The entity – christened 'George' – is said to haunt the stockroom, where heavy bins were reportedly tipped over by an unseen force; stockroom workers told the newspaper that they had been prodded and bumped into by the same entity. Towards the end of 2004, the sensation that 'something' was in the stockroom was beginning to unnerve workers, who reported seeing something shadowy out the corner of their eyes. It moved quickly around the place and its appearances seemed to be becoming more frequent.

Although the Index store was a new building, it was located in the vicinity of a sixteenth-century monastery that stood on Freshney Place.

On Cleethorpes Road can be found Beagles Lighting. On Saturday 28 May 2005, investigators from the television show *Most Haunted* joined the list of paranormal researchers, mediums and even a shamanic pathwalker, who had investigated the mysterious goings-on at Beagles Lighting.

Since moving in seven months previously, shop owner Fiona Glover had had to put up with doors opening and slamming on their own accord – which would often trigger an alarm. Bulbs were repeatedly found unscrewed from lamps, lights dropped from the ceiling and boxes in the storeroom were thrown about during the night. Ghostly footsteps have also been reported. Ms Glover was forced to finally get help after a customer watched some unseen force throw a collection of candle shades across the shop floor.

Investigators from the Lincolnshire and East Riding Paranormal Investigation Team were brought in and they declared the place haunted. Mediums have sensed that there may be three spirits haunting the place: two men and a woman. One of the men has been 'felt' to be aggressive, and that he comes into the shop after drinking in the Albion public house over the road. He has then been 'sensed' to go upstairs and may have murdered his wife.

Ms Glover and employee Sandra Keogh have unearthed evidence as to the building's past life. In 1935 it was a radio factory; in 1910 it had been the Labour Exchange. Before that it had been Gooseman, the winemakers, but the two women have not been able to find out what the building was used as prior to this.

On Saturday 18 June 2005, the *Most Haunted* team transferred their attention to the National Fishing Heritage Centre, on Alexandra Dock, Grimsby. Here, visitors can experience every facet of the hardy life of the trawler man, with simulations of engine rooms, 1950s Grimsby and the vast North Atlantic fishing locations. There is even a real trawler docked nearby, the *Ross Tiger*.

But visitors and staff alike have reported that there is a strange presence within the attraction. In a simulation of a trawler's radio room there have been unexplained temperature drops and cold spots that are so extreme that people begin shivering. And the smell of strong tobacco has sometimes found its way into a room where no one is allowed to smoke. According to museum technician Pete Goodings, the source of the tobacco smell is a complete mystery.

Strange goings on were reported from within the trawler *Ross Tiger* as well. Visitors in the cabins have heard the sound of heavy footsteps thumping on deck when there was no one there, and a door which was always kept open was found to be jammed shut.

Those at the National Fishing Heritage Centre are not afraid of the spectre, and over the two years of reported paranormal activity they have come to accept him. They believe that he may be the ghost of a former skipper of the *Ross Tiger*, who has – rather aptly – come ashore and now haunts the maritime museum. Culture manager Chris Jones said, 'We all feel it's the right place for him to be and feel comforted that he is still with us.'

Mac Peace in Scunthorpe

Ghost hunter Andrew Green, who died in 2005, collected many tales of the supernatural – including one about Scunthorpe General Hospital. This phantom would usually appear when a baby at the hospital was seriously ill. The first sign that the spiritual entity was around would be a strong scent of musty violet perfume. When the ghost appeared, it took the form of a nurse in a long skirt; afterwards, Green reported, the desperately ill infant would recover.

If the phantom still resides at the hospital then the curious wafts of violet fragrance may be a mystery to the staff these days. But Sandra Manning, of Winterton, recalled that the story of the mysterious nurse was well known when she worked there between 1969 and 1990. Back then the place was called the War Memorial Hospital, and the story went that the ghost worked on Ward 4 (then a children's ward). Although she never saw it herself, Sandra claimed there was an atmosphere that unnerved both her and her colleagues, and any strange noises so frightened the nurses that they refused to take their second breaks alone in the evenings. Sandra remembered that the ghostly nurse had allegedly been a cancer victim in life.

Another former nurse, Lorna Pearcey, of Scunthorpe, remembered how they had nicknamed the ghost Mac Peace. Former nightshift staff nurse Sheila Caine, remembers hearing that Mac Peace's real name had been Bertha, and that she had been a very short, slight lady. Bertha had died from cancer in 1960 or 1961, but in life she always wore sweet smelling violet-scented perfume and worked the corridor between Roadley and Cliff Wards. Sheila had also heard how, after her death, Mac Peace was supposed to have appeared, smelling of violets, in the presence of a seriously ill child. It was also rumoured that the spirit had been spied feeding a baby.

A hospital spokesperson, Lisa Webster, denied that there was a perfume-scented angel of mercy floating round the wards and corridors of Scunthorpe General Hospital. But it would seem that the tale was well known amongst the floor staff in the years following Mac Peace's death in the early 1960s.

The tale of the phantom nurse elicited fascination amongst the readership of the *Scunthorpe Telegraph*, and amongst the correspondents who contacted the paper was Sheila Peace, who said she was the daughter-in-law of Mac Peace. Her mother-in-law's maiden name was Bertha Gertrude Hamilton MacHarry and she had married the late Harry Peace – hence the explanation for her nickname. Bertha was buried in Brumby cemetery, Scunthorpe.

Sheila Peace had been unaware of her mother-in-law's strange legacy at the hospital until she herself was staying there during the birth of her own daughter in 1978; it was then that a nurse casually mentioned the ghost of Ward 4 and who it was supposed to be! Sheila was dumbfounded by the story.

State registered nurse Linda Kidd told the *Scunthorpe Telegraph* that the 'old' Ward 11 was supposed to echo to the sounds of a child crying. The child had died, and perhaps this is what Mac Peace wants so desperately to stop from happening again…

On 30 April 2005 the *Scunthorpe Telegraph* carried a report concerning the experiences of Diane Hudomiet, which seemed to bear out the stories that – apart from the phantom nurse – ghostly children also inhabited Scunthorpe General Hospital. During her seven years employment at the hospital, Mrs Hudomiet had worked in the intensive care unit for fifteen months. According to Mrs Hudomiet, the old children's ward was allegedly haunted by a little girl who could be found near the bathroom at the end of the ward. The little girl had her long blonde hair in plaits and she would ask to use the toilet. After being taken to the toilet she would mysteriously vanish.

Scunthorpe General Hospital

Perhaps this blonde girl and the crying child mentioned earlier are one and the same? Mrs Hudomiet told the *Telegraph* that she recalled one poignant incident when a young girl was brought into the intensive care unit after being involved in a road accident. Mrs Hudomiet said, 'It was very rare any children were in the unit. Sick children always pull at the heartstrings, touching every member of staff and causing emotion to come to the surface.'

Yet on the day the little girl was taken to theatre, Mrs Hudomiet and a colleague heard children laughing and playing: it sounded as though they were in a playground, rather than a hospital!

Sadly, the little girl died. Although Mrs Hudomiet had not been on duty, she recalled that the following morning staff reported that they had heard the distressing sound of children weeping on the unit.

Mrs Hudomiet also recalled a male patient sitting up in bed after an operation, who claimed to see a small boy aged about six or seven; the lad had short dark hair and the patient could 'see' him sitting on an empty chair next to Mrs Hudomiet and one of her colleagues. Of course the two staff nurses could see nobody, and the incident spooked them for a while.

In such places as hospitals, where action, relief and trauma jostle for space it is perhaps not surprising that these types of stories abound. But quite why such legends should be common currency at Scunthorpe General Hospital and not other hospitals in the county remains an eerie mystery.

Other local titles published by Tempus

Lincoln History & Guide

MICHAEL J. JONES

Lincoln was a major centre under Roman, Viking and medieval rule and each of these areas has left its mark on the city. The cathedral and the castle were built in the years following the Norman Conquest, the cathedral becoming one of Britain's finest examples of Early English Gothic architecture. This volume is a well illustrated and readable introduction to the city's past that will appeal to residents and visitors alike.

0 7524 3389 X

Shipping on the Humber: The South Bank

MIKE TAYLOR

The River Humber has been used for commercial navigation for centuries and remains one of the busiest waterways in Britain. This collection of images, dating from the late nineteenth century to the present day, explores the South Bank of the river, travelling topographically from Louth and Cleethorpes upriver to the Ouse/Trent confluence. The illustrations feature keels, sloops, lighters and motor barges, small craft such as dredgers and cross river ferries, as well as images of the docks and waterways themselves.

0 7524 2780 6

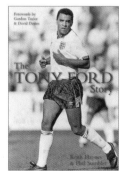

Trawlers of Humberside

R.F. ROBERTS

Fishing in Humberside was a large and lucrative business. During the peak years of the trawling industry, Grimsby was one of the three main fishing ports in the British Isles. Illustrated with over 100 old photographs, this book reveals the concise history of each craft and the crew of many of the trawlers that sailed from Humberside, as well as reports of sinkings or other disasters.

0 7524 3167 6

The Tony Ford Story

KEITH HAYNES AND PHIL SUMBLER

Having been in the game since 1974, when he made his debut for Grimsby Town, Tony Ford holds the record for the most appearances of any player in the history of British football. A black player plying his trade in the early 1970s and '80s, he rose above the abuse from opposing players and fans to forge a successful career as a player and a manager. This authorised biography, written in conjunction with Tony himself, is a great read for anyone with an interest in British football.

0 7524 2418 1

If you are interested in purchasing other books published by Tempus, or in case you have difficulty finding any Tempus books in your local bookshop, you can also place orders directly through our website

www.tempus-publishing.com